FLEX GRID TRANSFORMS ANIMATION SCSS

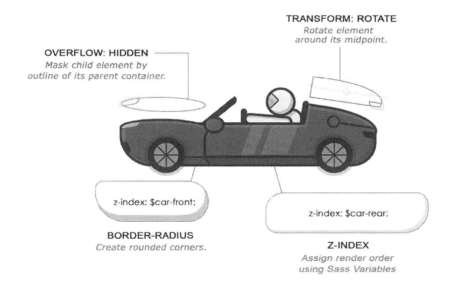

OVERFLOW: HIDDEN
Mask child element by outline of its parent container.

TRANSFORM: ROTATE
Rotate element around its midpoint.

z-index: $car-front;

BORDER-RADIUS
Create rounded corners.

z-index: $car-rear;

Z-INDEX
Assign render order using Sass Variables

Learning Curve Books ™

Title:	CSS – Visual Dictionary
Edition:	I – June 1, 2018
Genre:	Web Design & UI Design
Publisher:	Learning Curve Books
Imprint:	Independently published
ISBN:	9781983065637
Author:	Greg Sidelnikov (greg.sidelnikov@gmail.com)

Editors, volunteers, contributors: Grace Neufeld, Sergio Martin, Katya Sorok, Sarah Chima, Audrey Delgado.

Primary purpose of **Learning Curve Books** publishing company is to provide *effective education* for web designers, software engineers and all readers who are interested in being edified in the area of web development.

This edition of **CSS – Visual Dictionary** was created to speed up the learning process of Cascading Style Sheets – a language for decorating HTML elements.

For questions and comments about the book you may contact the author or send an email directly to our office at the email address mentioned below.

Special Offers & Discounts Available
Schools, libraries and educational organizations may qualify for special prices. Get in touch with our distribution department at **hello@learningcurvebook.net**

Learning Curve Books™

Learning Curve Books is trademark of Learning Curve Books, LLC – an independent book publisher. License is required to distribute this volume in any form regardless of format. All graphics and content is copyright of Learning Curve Books, LLC. unless where otherwise stated.

©2018 – 2019 **Learning Curve Books, LLC.**

Contents

1 CSS Properties and Values   **1**
    1.1 External Placement 2
    1.2 Internal Placement 3
    1.3 Inline Placement 4
    1.4 CSS Grammar – Selector Syntax 5
    1.5 Relationship Between Properties & Values 11
    1.6 CSS Comments 12
    1.7 Assignment Patterns 14
    1.8 CSS Variables 16
       1.8.1 Local Variables 16
    1.9 Syntactically Awesome Stylesheets 17
    1.10 The Idea Behind Cascading Style Sheets 19
    1.11 CSS Selectors 22
    1.12 Forgiving Nature 22
    1.13 Common 22
    1.14 Shorthand Properties 23

2 Pseudo Elements   **24**
    2.1 ::after 24
    2.2 ::before 24
    2.3 ::first-letter 24
    2.4 ::first-line 24
    2.5 ::selection 24
    2.6 ::slotted(*) 25

3 Pseudo Selectors 25

3.1 :link 27

3.2 :visited 27

3.3 :hover 27

3.4 :active 28

3.5 :focus 28

3.6 :enabled 28

3.7 :disabled 28

3.8 :default 28

3.9 :indeterminate 29

3.10 :required 29

3.11 :optional 29

3.12 :read-only 29

3.13 :root 29

3.14 :only-of-type 30

3.15 :first-of-type 30

3.16 :nth-of-type() 30

3.17 :last-of-type 31

3.18 :nth-child() 31

3.19 :nth-last-child() 31

3.20 :nth-child(odd) 32

3.21 :nth-child(even) 32

3.22 :not() 32

3.23 :empty 32

3.24 :Nesting pseudo-selectors 33

3.25 :dir(rtl) and :dir(ltr) 33

	3.26 :only-child	33

4 CSS Box Model — 35

5 Position — 40
    5.1 Test Element 40
    5.2 static & relative 41
    5.3 absolute & fixed 43
    5.4 fixed 46
    5.5 sticky 47

6 Working With Text — 48
    6.1 Text Align 51
    6.2 Text Align Last 52
    6.3 Overflow 54
    6.4 Skip Ink 56
    6.5 Text Rendering 57
    6.6 Text Indent 58
    6.7 Text Orientation 59
    6.8 Text Shadow 62

7 Margin, Rounded Corners, Box Shadow and Z-Index — 65
    7.1 Border Radius 65

8 Nike Logo — 73

9 Display — 76

10 Element Visibility — 79

11 Floating Elements   80

12 Color Gradients   81
    12.1 Overview 82
    12.2 Gradient Types 85

13 Filters   91
    13.1 **blur()** 91
    13.2 **brightness()** 92
    13.3 **contrast()** 92
    13.4 **grayscale()** 92
    13.5 **hue-rotate()** 92
    13.6 **invert()** 93
    13.7 **opacity()** 93
    13.8 **saturate()** 93
    13.9 **sepia()** 93
    13.10 **drop-shadow()** 93

14 Background Images   94
    14.1 Specifying Multiple Values 100
    14.2 background-position 100
    14.3 Multiple Backgrounds 102
    14.4 Image Transparency 103
    14.5 Multiple Backgrounds 104
    14.6 background-attachment 107
    14.7 background-origin 108

15 object-fit — 110

16 Borders — 111
16.1 Elliptical Border Radius — 114

17 2D Transforms — 117
17.1 translate — 117
17.2 rotate — 117
17.3 transform-origin — 120

18 3D Transforms — 121
18.1 rotateX — 121
18.2 rotateY and rotateZ — 122
18.3 scale — 122
18.4 translate — 123
18.5 Creating A 3D Cube — 124

19 Flex — 126
19.1 display:flex — 126
19.2 Main-axis and Cross-axis — 126
19.3 Direction — 128
19.4 Wrap — 128
19.5 Flow — 129
19.6 justify-content: *value* — 132
19.7 align-items — 135
19.8 flex-basis — 136
19.9 flex-grow — 136

19.10 flex-shrink 137

19.11 order 138

19.12 justify-items 139

19.13 Interactive Flex Editor 140

20 CSS Grid — 141

20.1 CSS Grid Model 141

21 CSS Grid – Using Template Areas — 142

21.1 CSS Grid & Media Queries 145

    21.1.1 Media Queries 145

    21.1.2 Changing content based on browser size . . . 145

21.2 Creating Your First CSS Grid 147

21.3 Implicit Rows and Columns 150

21.4 grid-auto-rows 153

21.5 Automatic Column Cell Width 154

21.6 Gaps 155

21.7 fr – Fractional Unit – for efficiently sizing the remaining space. 161

21.8 Working With Fractional Units 163

22 Fractional Units & Gaps — 166

22.1 Repeating Values 169

22.2 Spans 170

22.3 Start and End 174

22.4 Start and End's Shorthand 178

22.5 Content Align Within CSS Grid Items 181

22.6 align-self 181

  22.7 justify-self 183
  22.8 Template Areas 184
  22.9 Naming Grid Lines 186

23 Animation   189
  23.1 animation 191
  23.2 animation-name 192
  23.3 animation-duration 192
  23.4 animation-delay 193
  23.5 animation-direction 194
  23.6 animation-iteration-count 195
  23.7 animation-timing-function 196
  23.8 animation-fill-mode 200
  23.9 animation-play-state 201

24 Forward & Inverse Kinematics   202

25 Sassy CSS / SCSS Manual   203
  25.1 New Syntax 203
  25.2 Prerequisites 204
  25.3 Superset 205
  25.4 Variables 205
  25.5 Nested Rules 206
  25.6 The & character 207
  25.7 Mixins 208
  25.8 Multiple Browsers Example 208
  25.9 Arithmetic Operators 209

- 25.9.1 Addition 209
- 25.9.2 Subtraction 210
- 25.9.3 Multiplication 210
- 25.9.4 Division 210
- 25.9.5 Remainder 211
- 25.9.6 Comparison Operators 213
- 25.9.7 Logical Operators 214
- 25.9.8 Strings 215
- 25.10 Control-Flow Statements 216
  - 25.10.1 **if()** 217
  - 25.10.2 **@if** 217
  - 25.10.3 **@for** 220
  - 25.10.4 **@each** 220
  - 25.10.5 **@while** 221
- 25.11 Sass Functions 222
- 25.12 Sass Trigonometry 223
- 25.13 Writing your own functions in Sass 223
- 25.14 Oscillator Animation 226

26 Tesla CSS Art   229

CSS Visual Dictionary

Several months have gone into creation of the book you are holding in your hands (or on your device) right now. Indeed, ***CSS – Visual Dictionary*** is a work of love and hard labor. Thoughtfully created to help maximize your journey on your way to expanding your knowledge of CSS – Cascading Style Sheets. A language for decorating HTML elements.

We hope that this volume will serve as a faithful guide on your desk in the years to come.

1 CSS Properties and Values

On June 1st 2018, CSS had **415** unique properties attached to `style` object on any element in Chrome browser. As of December 21st there are **522** unique properties. In just 7 months, Chrome added over 100 new properties. This will happen many times again as CSS specification continues to evolve.

How many properties are present in your browser as of today? You can verify this yourself with a simple *JavaScript* code snippet as follows:

```
001  // Create a new HTML element
002  let element = document.createElement("div");
003
004  let p = 0; // Create counter
005  for (index in element.style)
006      p++;
007
008  // Outputs 522 in Chrome as of December 21st, 2018
009  console.log( p );
```

Figure 1: To list all CSS properties available in your browser, run this JavaScript code (***codepen.io*** *is the quickest way to test CSS and JavaScript*). Results may vary across different browsers and versions.

To make this book, all properties were printed out and organized by primary category (*position*, *dimension*, *layouts*, **CSS Animation**, etc.) Then, a diagram for every property that renders or modifies visual output, in some important way, was created with a brief description of the accompanying property name and value.

Large number of CSS properties rarely in use (*or the ones that still don't have full browser support across all major browsers*) were skipped from the contents of this book. They would only create unneeded clutter.

Instead, the content will focus only on properties that are in common use by web designers and developers today. A great deal of effort went into creation of **CSS Grid** and **Flex** diagrams. A brief manual on **Sass/SCSS** was also included, but only most relevant features you should know about were chosen.

1.1 External Placement

CSS code can be saved in a separate, external file (`style.css`, in this example) and included as follows using the HTML `link` tag:

```
001  body p
002  {
003      background: white;
004      color: black;
005      font-family: Arial, sans-serif;
006      font-size: 16px;
007      line-height: 1.58;
008      text-rendering: optimizeLegibility;
009      -webkit-font-smoothing: antialiased;
010  }
```

Figure 2: Source code listing for `style.css` file.

```
001  <html>
002      <head>
003          <title>Welcome to my website.</title>
004          <link rel = "stylesheet"
005                type = "text/css"
006                href = "style.css" />
007      </head>
008      <body>
009          <p>CSS style instructions stored in
010  "style.css" will be applied to the content on
011  this page.</p>
012      </body>
013  </html>
```

Figure 3: Example of linking to an external CSS file.

1.2 Internal Placement

Or you can type it directly into your HTML document between two **style** tags, as shown in the following example:

```
001  <html>
002    <head>
003      <style type = "text/css">
004        body p
005        {
006            background: white;
007            color: black;
008            font-family: Arial, sans-serif;
009            font-size: 16px;
010            line-height: 1.58;
011            text-rendering: optimizeLegibility;
012            -webkit-font-smoothing: antialiased;
013        }
014      </style>
015    </head>
016    <body>
017      <p>CSS instructions specified above in the
018  style tag will be applied to this HTML paragraph
019  tag.</p>
020    </body>
021  </html>
```

Figure 4: You can place CSS inside **style** tags on the same HTML page.

1.3 Inline Placement

```
001  <html>
002    <head></head>
003    <body style = "font-family: Arial;">
004      <p>When outputted in browser, this
005  paragraph will inherit Arial font from inline
006  definition in its parent tag.</p>
007    </body>
008  </html>
```

Figure 5: Inline placement of HTML code using `style` attribute on an HTML element.

1.4 CSS Grammar – Selector Syntax

We now understand where CSS code is placed within an HTML document.

But before we go into visualizing each individual property it's good to become familiar with the grammar of CSS language – the syntax rules for specifying properties and values.

The most common selector is the HTML *tag name* itself.

Using the *tag name* will produce a selection of *all* elements of that type:

```
001  body { /* CSS properties go here */ }
```

Figure 6: Let's select the `<body>` tag by its name.

At first sight, because there is only one body tag in an HTML document, it's the only thing that will be selected.

But because of cascading nature of CSS, any property we add between the brackets, will also apply to all of its descendants (*children elements contained within the body tag, even if we don't explicitly specify their style.*)

This is an empty selector. It selects the body tag, but doesn't assign any properties to it yet.

Here are a few other examples of selecting elements by their HTML tag name. This is as common as you can get.

```
001  /* Select all paragraph <p> tags */
002  p { }
003
004  /* Select all <div> tags */
005  div { }
006
007  /* Select all <p> tags only if they are in <div> tags */
008  div p { }
```

Figure 7: Select some paragraph tags.

Your actual CSS commands will go inside the `{ ...here... }` brackets.

A CSS command consists of the ***selector*** and a `property: value;` pair. Multiple properties must be separated by *semicolon*. Let's start with single property, just to see how CSS property syntax works:

```
001  <div id = "box">content<div>
```

Figure 8: An HTML element with `id` attribute set to `"box"`.

In CSS `id` becomes the number character # aka *hashtag*:

```
001  #box { property: value; }
```

Use `id` to label elements whenever you have a completely *unique* container.

Do not name every single HTML element using an `id`, but reserve it for naming global parent elements or for elements that do something significant (for example, elements that often need to be updated with new content.).

What if we want to select more than one element at the same time?

```
001  <ul>
002      <li class = "item">1<li>
003      <li class = "item">2<li>
004      <li class = "item">3<li>
005  </li>
```

Likewise, the `class` attribute becomes dot (.) selector:

```
001  .item { line-height: 1.80; }
```

In this example, the dot character is used to select multiple elements sharing the same class name, and set a `line-height` to value of `1.50` (*which will result in a value roughly 150% of the font's height.*).

Specifying CSS rules within `:root` selector will apply them to all ***all*** HTML elements. You can use `:root` to set *default* CSS values to entire document.

```
001 :root { font-family: Arial, sans-serif; }
```

Figure 9: Set *Arial* as the default font for entire document or gracefully degrade to *sans-serif* if Arial is not available. You can specify as many fonts as you want, separated by comma.

The `:root` selector is also often used to *globally* store CSS variables:

```
001 :root { --red-color: red; }
```

Figure 10: Create a new CSS variable called `--red-color` and assign CSS color value of `red` to it.

All CSS variable names must begin with double dash `--`.

```
001 div { color: var(--red-color); }
```

Figure 11: Now you can use this CSS variable `--red-color` as a value in your standard CSS selectors.

We've just explored how `:root` selector can help us store CSS variables and that it can also create a default *document-wide* CSS reset.

The star selector does the same thing:

```
001 * { font-family: Arial, sans-serif; }
```

Figure 12: It's possible to use the star (*) selector to the same effect as `:root`. The only difference is that star selector selects absolutely all elements in the document, but `:root` selects *only* the document container without its children.

Even though the star selector yields the same effect, it's less proper to use it for applying styles to the entire document (use `:root` instead).

The star selector is best reserved for selecting a batch of "all elements" within a specific parent element:

```
001  <div id = "parent">
002      <div>A</div>
003      <div>B</div>
004      <ul>
005          <li>1</li>
006          <li>2</li>
007      </ul>
008      <p>Text.</p>
009  </div>
```

Figure 13: `#parent *` selector can be used to select all children of a parent element, regardless of their type.

As you continue to experiment with selectors you will notice that it's possible to select the same HTML elements using different *combinations* of selectors.

For example, the following combinations all select exactly the same set of elements (all children of the parent element, excluding the parent itself):

```
001  /* Select all children of #parent */
002  #parent * { color: blue; }
003
004  /* Combine multiple selectors using comma */
005  #parent div,
006  #parent ul,
007  #parent p { color: blue; }
008
009  /* Using :nth-child pseudo-selectors */
010  #parent nth-child(1),
011  #parent nth-child(2),
012  #parent nth-child(3),
013  #parent nth-child(4) { color: blue; }
```

Figure 14: `#parent *` selector can be used to select all children of a parent element, regardless of their type.

Of course, just because you can, doesn't mean you should. This is only an example.

The most elegant solution in this case is `#parent *`

But each coding situation, website or application call for a layout unique to its structure and purpose.

Crafting selectors might sound like a simple task at first. But not until you delve into more complex UI cases.

With time, your CSS code will continue to become more complex.

Complexity of CSS code is tightly coupled with the structure of the HTML document itself.

Therefore, even some of the most clever selectors can often "intersect" with selectors created in the future, creating conflicts. It's a bit of an art to handle CSS gracefully. An improvement to your CSS selector creation skills can be observed only after long hours of practice!

In production environment working on a real project, you won't be able to count how many times you **will** find yourself in a situation when changing a CSS property no longer produces the desired result, due to growing complexity of the application layout.

Looking at the screen for hours, baffled at why something isn't working as it should, you will often find yourself in this situation when working with Cascading Style Sheets.

When a particular use-case is overlooked and a mistake is made, developers often use `!important` keyword as a quick fix.

You can override any CSS style by appending *!important* keyword to the end of your CSS statement:

```
001  /* Select all children of #parent */
002  #parent * { color: blue; }
003
004  /* Select only div in #parent and change color to red */
005  #parent div { color: red; }
006
007  /* Make sure all div's are green in entire document */
008  div { color: green !important; }
```

Figure 15: It's tempting to use `!important` keyword to force-set CSS style. But it's usually considered a bad practice, defying the cascading logic of the style sheets!

A word of caution. It is recommended to avoid *!important* directive at all costs. Even though it may seem like you are fixing the problem, it can result in making your CSS code even more rigid and difficult to maintain.

Ideally, you want to keep your CSS selectors as simple and effective as possible. This isn't always an easy balance to keep.

I usually start by plan my CSS code on a sheet of paper. Spending a bit more time thinking through the structure of your application and making mental notes goes a long way when designing better selectors.

1.5 Relationship Between Properties & Values

Not all CSS properties are made alike.

Depending on the property type, the value can be a **measure of space** specified in *pixels*, *pt*, *em* or *fr* units, a **color** in named (*red*, *blue*, *black*, etc...,) hexadecimal (*#0F0* or *#00FF00*...) or rgb(*r, g, b*) formats.

Other times the value is unique to a specific property name that cannot be used with any other property. For example, the CSS `transform` property can take a value specified using `rotate` keyword. It takes an ***angle*** in degrees – here, CSS requires that you append `deg` to the numeric degree value:

```
001  /* rotate this element by 45 degrees in
002      clock-wise direction */
003
004  #box {
005      transform: rotate(45deg);
006  }
```

But it's not the only way to specify a rotation angle.

CSS offers 3 other ***types*** of units specifically for rotation: `grad`, `rad` and `turn`.

```
001  /* 200 Gradians (Also called gons or grades.) */
002  transform: rotate(200grad);
003
004  /* 1.4 Radians */
005  transform: rotate(1.4rad);
006
007  /* 0.5 turns or 180 degrees (1 turn = 360 degrees) */
008  transform: rotate(0.5turn);
```

Figure 16: Here we are using `grad` (*Gradians*), `rad` (*Radians*), and `turn` *Turns* as an alternative way to specify rotation angle of an HTML element.

Alternative ways of specifying *values* are not uncommon to many other CSS properties. For example `#F00`, `#FF0000`, `red`, `rgb(255, 255, 255)` and `rgba(255, 255, 255, 1.0)` specify exactly the same color.

1.6 CSS Comments

CSS only supports "block comment" syntax for creating in-code comments. It's done by surrounding a block of text with `/* comment */` symbols.

```
001  /* Set font color to white using Hexadecimal value */
002  p { color: #FFFFFF; }
003
004  /* Set font color to white using short Hexadecimal value */
005  p { color: #FFF; }
006
007  /* Set font color to white using named value */
008  p { color: white; }
009
010  /* Set font color to white using an RGB value */
011  p { color: rgb(255,255,255); }
012
013  /* Create CSS variable --white-color (note double dash) */
014  :root { --white-color: rgba(255, 255, 255, 1.0); }
015
016  /* Set font color to white using a CSS variable */
017  p { color: var(--white-color); }
```

Figure 17: Note how the same property `color` can take different types of values. When using CSS variables, the variable name is preceded by a double dash –.

You can also comment out an entire section of CSS code:

```
001  /* Temporarily disable this CSS block
002      content:        "hello";
003      border:         1px solid gray;
004      color:          #FFFFFF;
005      line-height:    48px;
006      padding:        32px;
007  */
```

Figure 18: Temporary disable a block of CSS code, for testing new code or future reference, etc.

CSS does not support inline syntax // *inline comments are not allowed* or rather... it has no effect on the browser's CSS interpreter.

1.7 Assignment Patterns

There are many *dimension-* and *size-*related properties in CSS (`left`, `top`, `width` and `height` and many others.) It would be redundant to list them all here. Therefore, examples in this section will be using the word *property* to demonstrate the key `property:value` assignment patterns.

You can use `property:value` pair combination to set background images, colors and other basic properties of HTML elements.

You could alternatively use `property: value value value` to assign multiple values to a single property, to avoid redundant declarations. These are called **shorthands**. They usually separate multiple property values by space.

Without *shorthands* you would end up specifying each part of a property on a separate line:

```
/* background */
background-color:    black;
background-image:    url("image.jpg");
background-position: center;
background-repeat:   no-repeat;

/* shorthand, just one line of code! */
background: black url("image.jpg") center no-repeat;
```

But CSS has undergone considerable upgrades over the years. Before we begin exploring the visual diagrams describing each CSS property it is imperative to understand how CSS interprets property and value patterns.

The majority of properties use these patterns:

```
/* The most common pattern */
property: value;

/* values separated by space */
property: value value value;

/* values separated by comma */
property: value, value, value;
```

Size-related properties can be calculated using `calc` keyword:

```
001  /* calculated */
002  property: calc(valuepx);
003
004  /* calculated between % and px - ok. */
005  property: calc(value% - valuepx);
006
007  /* calculated between % and % -  ok. */
008  property: calc(value% - value%);
009
010  /* add px to px - ok. */
011  property: calc(valuepx + valuepx );
```

Subtraction, *multiplication* and *division* follow identical pattern. Just try not to divide by a `px` value:

```
001  /* subtract px from px - ok. */
002  property: calc(valuepx - valuepx);
003
004  /* multiply px by number - ok. */
005  property: calc(valuepx * number});
006
007  /* divide px by number - ok. */
008  property: calc(valuepx / number});
009
010  /* divide number by px - error. */
011  property: calc(number / valuepx});
```

The last example will produce an error. When using `calc` you cannot divide a *number* by a value specified in pixels (*px*).

1.8 CSS Variables

You can use CSS variables to avoid defining the same values multiple times in different CSS selectors. CSS variable names always begin with a double dash -- sequence.

```
/* define variable --default-color */
:root { --default-color: yellow; }

/* define variable --variable-name */
:root { --variable-name: 100px; }

/* set background color to --default-color variable */
element { background-color: var(--default-color); }

/* set width to 100px */
element { width: var(--variable-name); }
```

Figure 19: To define a CSS variable in global scope, use :root selector. Here *element* is used only as a placeholder, in a real case scenario, it would be replaced with a valid HTML tag name.

1.8.1 Local Variables

You can create local variables, to be contained within a specific parent element only. This way they don't leak out into *global scope* and get mangled with other variable definitions that can potentially be declared using the same name.

```
// Define a local variable
.notifications { --notification-color: blue; }

// Localize the variable to children elements
.notifications div {
  color: var(--notification-color);
  border: 1px solid var(--notification-color);
}
```

Figure 20: It's a good idea to keep variable definitions concealed to the *scope* in which they are used. This is generally a good practice to follow in any programming language, such as JavaScript, but also CSS.

1.9 Syntactically Awesome Stylesheets

Syntactically Awesome Stylesheet or **SASS** for short is a CSS preprocessor that adds new features not currently available in standard CSS specification.

SASS is a superset of standard CSS. This means everything that works in CSS will work in SASS.

We no longer use the older SASS syntax with file extension `.sass`.

Instead `.scss` is used – a more recent (*and better*) version of SASS.

SCSS is recommended for advanced CSS specialists. Perhaps, someone who can appreciate the beauty of using a for-loop as a CSS style directive.

Note, that as of December 10th, 2018, Sass/SCSS will not work out of the box in any browser. You need to install Sass compiler from the command line in order to enable it on your web server.

If you want to start experimenting with Sass, head over to `www.codepen.io` where you can readily start using the Sass interpreted without any preliminary setup. **CodePen** is a social development environment for front-end designers and developers.

```
001  $font: Helvetica, sans-serif;
002  $dark-gray: #333;
003
004  body {
005     font: 16px $font;
006     color: $dark-gray;
007  }
```

Figure 21: SASS variable names are defined with a leading $ character, similar to PHP language!

What kind of things can be done using SASS?

```
001  $a: #E50C5E;
002  $b: #E16A2E;
003
004  .mixing-colors {
005      background-color: mix($a, $b, 30%);
006  }
```

Figure 22: Here, SASS was used to mix two colors defined in SASS variables $a and $b.

I encourage you to further study Sass/SCSS on your own, but only once you feel comfortable with standard CSS described in this book!

1.10 The Idea Behind Cascading Style Sheets

Cascading Style Sheets are named this way for a reason. Imagine a waterfall with water running down, breaking against the stones beneath. Every one of those stones on which the water fell becomes wet. Similarly, every CSS style inherits the styles already applied to its parent HTML element.

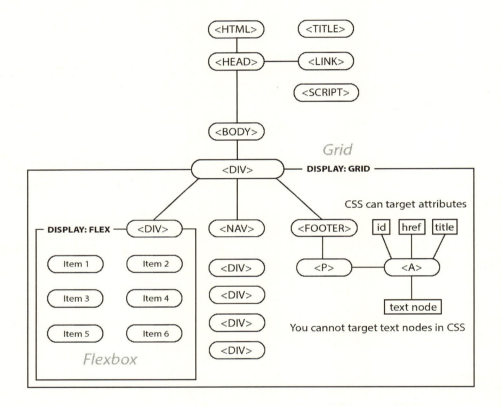

Figure 23: CSS selectors help traverse the Document Object Model.

CSS styles literally "trickle down" the DOM hierarchy, consisting of a tree-like structure of your website. The CSS language (specifically, by providing a number of CSS *selectors*) gives you ability to control this often quirky process.

Let's take a look at this simple website structure to demonstrate the basic concept behind CSS:

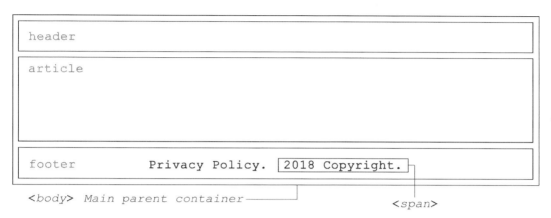

Figure 24: A few elements nested within the main website container. CSS is a lot like a pair of tweezers, that helps us pick elements we want to apply a certain style to.

If you apply black background to <body> tag then all of the nested elements within it will automatically inherit a black background:

```
1  body { background: black color: white; };
```

This style will "cascade" down the parent hierarchy, making all of the following HTML elements inherit white text on black background:

```
001  <body>
002    <header>
003      <p>Website header</p>
004    </header>
005    <article>
006      <p>Main content</p>
007    </article>
008    <footer>
009      <p>Privacy Policy. <span>&copy; 2019 Copyright</span></p>
010    </footer>
011  </body>
```

Figure 25: Basic HTML structure.

If you want to single out the footer and highlight the word *Privacy Policy* in **red** color and *2018 Copyright* in **green** color, you can expand on the cascading principle further by applying these CSS commands:

```
001  body            { background: black; color: white; }
002  footer          { color: red; }
003  footer span     { color: green; }
```

Figure 26: Basic CSS commands.

Note that there is a space between footer and span. In CSS, a space is an actual CSS selector character. It means: "find within of the previously specified tag" (which is "footer" in this example.)

1.11 CSS Selectors

```
/* Select a single element whose id attribute is "id" */
#id { }

/* Select all elements whose class name is "class1" */
.class { }

/* Select all elements whose class name is "class1" cascading
    under another parent element whose id is "parent" */
#parent .class1 {  }
```

Figure 27: Basic CSS selectors.

1.12 Forgiving Nature

Because it was designed for environments where downloading the full copy of a website is not always guaranteed, CSS is one of the most forgiving languages, similar to HTML. If you make mistakes, or for some reason the page didn't finish loading completely, CSS code will degrade gracefully to as much as it *can* interpret. Ironically, this means you can still use the // ***inline comments*** but you probably shouldn't.

1.13 Common

Some of the most common CSS property and value combinations: t

```
/* Set font color to white */
color: #FFFFFF;

/* Set background color to black */
background-color: #000000;

/* Create 1px-thick blue border around the element */
border: 1px solid blue;
```

```
001  /* Set font color to white */
002  font-family: Arial, sans-serif;
003
004  /* Set font size to 16px */
005  font-size: 16px;
006
007  /* Add padding of 32px thickness in size */
008  padding: 32px;
009
010  /* Add 16px of margin space around content area */
011  margin: 16px;
```

1.14 Shorthand Properties

Let's assign 3 different properties that contribute to the appearance of the background image of an HTML element:

```
001  background-color: #000000;
002  background-image: url("image.jpg");
003  background-repeat: no-repeat;
004  background-position: left top;
005  background-size: cover;
006  background-atachment: fixed;
```

The same can be rewritten by using a single *shorthand* property `background`, separated by space:

background: background-color background-image background-repeat;

(And the rest of background combinations: they can all be found in the Backgrounds chapter.)

```
001  background: #000000 url("image.jpg") left top no-repeat fixed;
```

Shorthands also exist on various **CSS Grid** and **Flex** properties.

2 Pseudo Elements

Pseudo elements start with double colon ::. Here, *pseudo* simply means that they don't refer to the explicit DOM elements you added to your HTML document by hand. For example the text selection element.

2.1 ::after

```
p::after { content: "Added After"; }
```

| `<p>` | One of the often overlooked features of CSS are the pseudo-element selectors. | `</p>` | Added After |

2.2 ::before

```
p::before { content: "Added Before"; }
```

| Added Before | `<p>` | One of the often overlooked features of CSS are the pseudo-element selectors. | `</p>` |

2.3 ::first-letter

```
p::first-letter { font-size: 200%; }
```

| `<p>` | **O**ne of the often overlooked features of CSS are the pseudo-element selectors. | `</p>` |

2.4 ::first-line

```
p::first-line { text-transform: uppercase; }
```

| `<p>` | THIS IS A LONG PARAGRAPH OF TEXT DEMONSTRATING HOW THE ::FIRST-LINE PSEUDO-ELEMENT affects only the first paragraph of text even if it's part of the same paragraph tag. | `</p>` |

2.5 ::selection

```
::selection { background: black; color: white; caret-color: blue; }
```

The ::selection pseudo-element is applied to text selection.

2.6 ::slotted(*)

Slotted pseudo selector works only in the context of the HTML `<template>` element, for selecting `<slots>`.

`::slotted(*)` or `::slotted(`*element-name*`)`

```
<template>
  <div>
    <slot name = "animal"></slot>
    <ul>
      <li><slot name = "kind">Cat</slot></li>
      <li><slot name = "name">Felix</slot></li>
    </ul>
  </div>
</template>
```

3 Pseudo Selectors

In CSS a **pseudo selector** is any selector that starts with a colon character (:) and is usually appended to the end of *another* element name – often a parent container. They are also known as **pseudo classes.**

Pseudo-selectors `:first-child` and `:last-child` are used for selecting the very *first* or very *last* element from a list of children in a parent.

Another example is `:nth-child` for selecting a series of elements belonging to a row or column in a list of elements or even an HTML table.

Let's take at a few cases that demonstrate the use of *pseudo-selectors*.

They are effective when used together in combination with other element selectors. By looking how pseudo selector affect an HTML table, it's easy to quickly understand how pseudo selectors work, because a table has children elements spanning in both dimensions (rows x columns).

You can use `table tr:first-child` to select all items on the first row:

Figure 28: table tr:first-child

Select the first column of every row using `table td:first-child` selector:

Figure 29: table td:first-child

(Notice there is no space between `td` and `:first-child`. This is important, because `td :first-child` (*with space*) is a completely different selector. The change is subtle but the results are different, as your result will be equivalent to `td *:first-child` instead.)

Remember how the *space character* itself is an element hierarchy selector? Examples below combine *pseudo selectors* with both `tr` and `td` to laser target a particular column or row:

Figure 30: table tr td:nth-child(2)

Figure 31: table tr:nth-child(2) td:nth-child(2)

Figure 32: table tr:nth-child(2)

Figure 33: table tr:last-child td:last-child

The same ***nth-child*** rules apply to all other *nested groups of elements*, like `ul` and `li` for example, and any other arbitrary parent/child combination.

Note that the ***space character*** itself is part of the selector. It helps you to drill down the hierarchy of parent elements.

3.1 :link

`:link` (the same as `a[href]`)

`<a href = "http://www.google.com/">Anchor text </a>`

`:link` does not select href-less a elements

`<a> href-less </a>`

3.2 :visited

`:visited` selects visited links in the current browser.

`<a href = "http://www.google.com/">Visited Link </a>`

3.3 :hover

`:hovered` selects link element hovered over by mouse cursor.

`<a href = "http://www.google.com/">Hovered Link </a>`

3.4 :active

`:active` selects an active or "pressed" link.

3.5 :focus

`:focus` selects elements with current focus, including links, input and textarea elements.

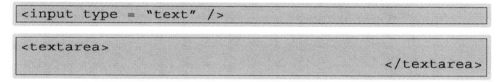

3.6 :enabled

`:enabled` Enabled elements can be activated (selected, clicked on, typed into) or accept focus. An element can also have a disabled state, in which it can't be activated or accept focus.

3.7 :disabled

`:disabled` Element can't be activated or accept focus. (Checkbox, or radio button for example.)

   `:checked` Checkbox or radio button.

3.8 :default

`input:default` Selects the default item in a form (checkbox or radio button)

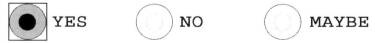

```
<form>
<input type = "radio" name = "answer" value - "YES" checked> YES</br>
<input type = "radio" name = "answer" value - "NO"> NO</br>
<input type = "radio" name = "answer" value - "MAYBE"> MAYBE</br>
</form>
```

3.9 :indeterminate

`:indeterminate` Checkbox or radio button that has not been assigned a default state..

3.10 :required

`:required` Selects input with the `required` attribute.

```
<input type = "text" required />
```

3.11 :optional

`:optional` Selects input without the `required` attribute.

```
<input type = "text" />
```

3.12 :read-only

`:read-only` and `read-write` selects elements with attributes `readonly` and `disabled`.

```
<input type = "text" disabled readonly />
```

3.13 :root

`:root` select root DOM element (`<html>`)

```
<html>                                                              </html>
```

3.14 :only-of-type

`li:only-of-type`

`<div>`						
	`<ul>`					
		`<li>`	`<span>`	Content.	`</span>`	`</li>`
		`<li>`	`<span>`	Content.	`</span>`	`</li>`
		`<li>`	`<span>`	Content.	`</span>`	`</li>`
	`</ul>`					
`</div>`						

3.15 :first-of-type

`div ul li:first-of-type`

`<div>`						
	`<ul>`					
		`<li>`	`<span>`	Content.	`</span>`	`</li>`
		`<li>`	`<span>`	Content.	`</span>`	`</li>`
		`<li>`	`<span>`	Content.	`</span>`	`</li>`
	`</ul>`					
`</div>`						

3.16 :nth-of-type()

`li:nth-of-type(2)`

`<div>`						
	`<ul>`					
		`<li>`	`<span>`	Content.	`</span>`	`</li>`
		`<li>`	`<span>`	Content.	`</span>`	`</li>`
		`<li>`	`<span>`	Content.	`</span>`	`</li>`
	`</ul>`					
`</div>`						

3.17 :last-of-type

```
div ul li:last-of-type
```

`<div>`						
	`<ul>`					
		`<li>`	`<span>`	Content.	`</span>`	`</li>`
		`<li>`	`<span>`	Content.	`</span>`	`</li>`
		`<li>`	`<span>`	Content.	`</span>`	`</li>`
	`</ul>`					
`</div>`						

3.18 :nth-child()

```
li:nth-child(1)
```

`<div>`						
	`<ul>`					
		`<li>`	`<span>`	Content.	`</span>`	`</li>`
		`<li>`	`<span>`	Content.	`</span>`	`</li>`
		`<li>`	`<span>`	Content.	`</span>`	`</li>`
	`</ul>`					
`</div>`						

3.19 :nth-last-child()

```
span:nth-last-child(1)
```

`<div>`						
	`<ul>`					
		`<li>`	`<span>`	Content.	`</span>`	`</li>`
		`<li>`	`<span>`	Content.	`</span>`	`</li>`
		`<li>`	`<span>`	Content.	`</span>`	`</li>`
	`</ul>`					
`</div>`						

3.20 :nth-child(odd)

`span:nth-child(odd)`

`<span>`	Content.	`</span>`
`<span>`	Content.	`</span>`
`<span>`	Content.	`</span>`
`<span>`	Content.	`</span>`

3.21 :nth-child(even)

`span:nth-child(even)`

`<span>`	Content.	`</span>`
`<span>`	Content.	`</span>`
`<span>`	Content.	`</span>`
`<span>`	Content.	`</span>`
`<span>`	Content.	`</span>`

3.22 :not()

`:not(.excluded)`

tr#first td	td.excluded
td.excluded	td.default
td.excluded	td.excluded
td.default	td.excluded

3.23 :empty

`p::first-line { text-transform: uppercase; }`

`<p>`	THIS IS A LONG PARAGRAPH OF TEXT DEMONSTRATING HOW THE ::FIRST-LINE PSEUDO-ELEMENT	
	affects only the first paragraph of text even if it's part of the same paragraph tag.	`</p>`

3.24 :Nesting pseudo-selectors

```
p:first-child:first-letter { font-size: 200%; }
```

| `<p>` | P seudo-selectors can be chained. | `</p>` |

3.25 :dir(rtl) and :dir(ltr)

`:dir(rtl)` or `:dir(ltr)`

```
<div dir = "rtl">Right to left</div>
<div dir = "ltr">Left to right</div>
<div dir = "auto">הבהא אוה םיהולא</div>
```

3.26 :only-child

`:only-child`

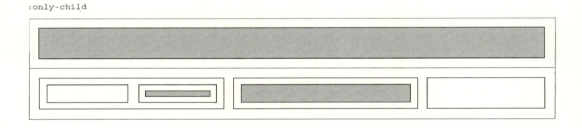

What if you need to select absolutely all elements on the page or within some parent element? No problem!

Figure 34: The star (*) selector selects all elements within a parent. In this case `table *` selector was used.

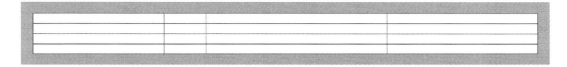

Figure 35: The difference between the star selector (*) and `:root`, is that `:root` only selects the main DOM container without children elements.

CSS language has changed over the years. In one of its more recent specifications, CSS draws a clear distinction between **Pseudo Selectors** (Which are also known as **Pseudo Classes**) and **Pseudo Elements** that start with double colon ::.

Pseudo Selectors / Classes usually select an existing element in the DOM whereas Pseudo Elements usually refer to elements not directly specified. For example, you can change the background color of a text selection, append content to imaginary `::before` and `::after` elements and few other things.

4 CSS Box Model

CSS *box model* is the fundamental structure of an HTML element. It consists of *content area* with 3 extra layers of space around it, namely: *padding*, *border* and a surrounding *margin* area.

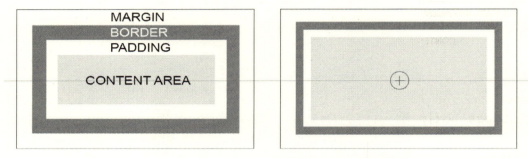

Figure 36: **Right:** The standard CSS box model includes a margin, border, padding and content area. If you plan on rotating an HTML element using the **transform** property, rotation will take place around center of the element, because it is by default as: **50% 50%**. Changing it to **0 0** will reset rotation point to upper left corner of the element.

The most important thing about the box model is that by default its `box-sizing` property is set to `content-box`. This works for text-based content, but I think it's a bit unfortunate for blocking elements in general, because this means adding padding, border or margin will change the *physical* dimensions of the blocking area. This is why CSS grid implements `border-box` by default. We will talk about CSS grid in a later chapter.

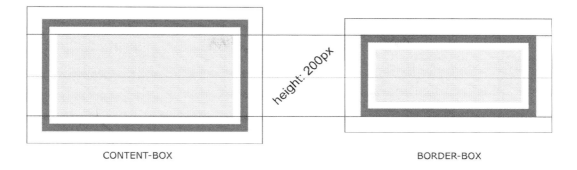

Figure 37: Note that the *value* 200px of the `height` property of the element does not change, but its physical dimensions do, based on `box-sizing: [content-box|padding-box|border-box]`

There is no `margin-box` because margins by definition surround a given content area.

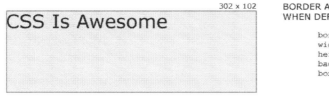

Figure 38: The `width` and `height` have increased by 2 pixels on each side because `1px` border was added to each of the 4 sides, when using default `content-box` model.

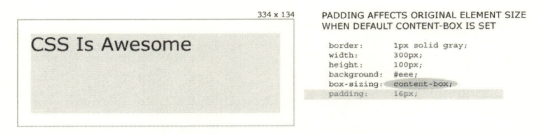

Figure 39: When both border and padding are present, the actual physical width becomes 334px x 134px. This is 34 pixels greater than the original dimensions (1px x 2 + 16px x 2 = 34px).

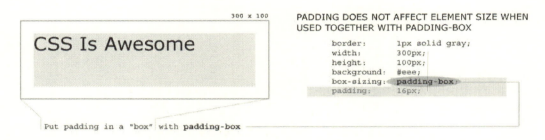

Figure 40: The `padding-box` value puts padding on the inside of content box. Now, the original dimensions are retained but the content is still padded.

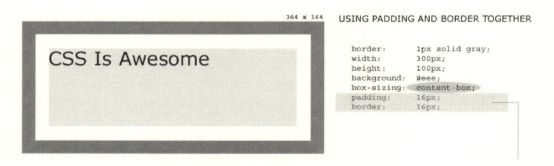

Figure 41: Here we overwrite the original value of `border: 1px solid gray` from previous example to `border: 16px` and together with `padding: 16px` the original width and height of the element are now padded by an extra 32px pixels on each side, adding a total of 64px to each dimension of the element.

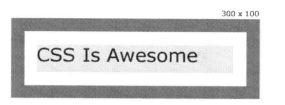

Figure 42: Using `border-box` will invert both the `border` and `padding` retaining original `width` and `height` of the element. This option is useful when you need to ensure your element will retain pixel-perfect dimensions, regardless of the size of its border or amount of padding.

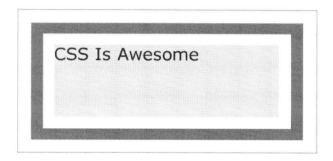

Figure 43: There is no `margin-box` in CSS, because margins by definition always refer to the space surrounding the content.

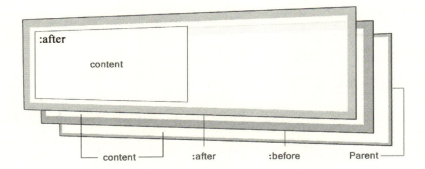

Figure 44: There is much more to a single HTML element than meets the eye.

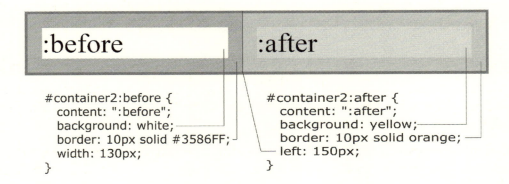

Figure 45: Both `:before` and `:after` elements are part of one single HTML element. You can even apply `position:absolute` to them and arrange them around without having to create any new elements!

5 Position

5.1 Test Element

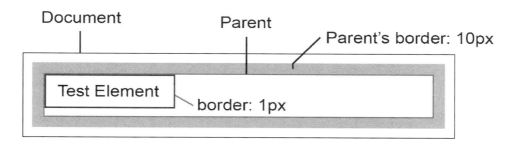

Figure 46: The following chapter on element position will use this specimen as an example.

Notice, there are actually 3 elements here. First is the document itself. But in theory it could be <html> or <body>, or any other parent container in isolation. The actual styles will be applied to the Test Element within that parent container.

Positioning elements in CSS may be affected by the properties of the parent container. To demonstrate various cases this particular setup will be helpful without having to display a complete website or application layout.

There are 5 available position types: `static` (*default*), `relative`, `absolute`, `fixed` and `sticky`. We'll explore them visually throughout this chapter.

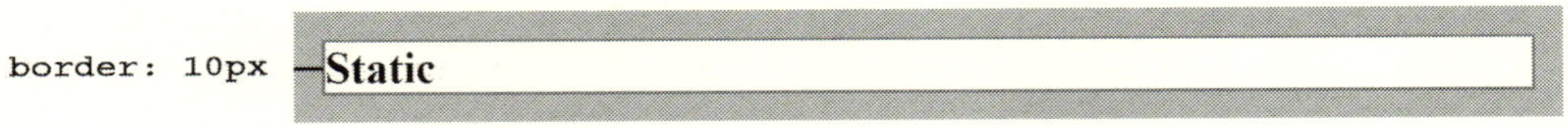

Figure 47: `static` is default for all elements.

Figure 48: `relative` is almost the same as static.

5.2 static & relative

By default `position` property is set to `static`, meaning the elements appear in the order they were specified in your HTML document, following normal HTML flow.

Statically positioned elements are not affected by `top`, `left`, `right` and `bottom` properties even if they are set to a value.

To demonstrate the difference, let's create some basic CSS styles:

```
001  /* Apply a border to all <div> elements */
002  div { border: 1px solid gray; }
003
004  /* Set some arbitrary width and position values */
005  #A { width: 100px; top: 25px; left: 100px; }
006  #B { width: 215px; top: 50px; }
007  #C { width: 250px; top: 50px; left: 25px; }
008  #D { width: 225px; top: 65px; }
009  #E { width: 200px; top: 70px; left: 50px; }
```

Figure 49: Let's define some CSS styles.

A border of `1px solid gray;` was applied to all `<div>` elements, so it makes it easier to see the actual dimensions of each HTML element when it's displayed in the browser.

On the next page we'll apply `position:static;` and `position:relative;` to the `<div>` element to see the difference between static and relative positioning.

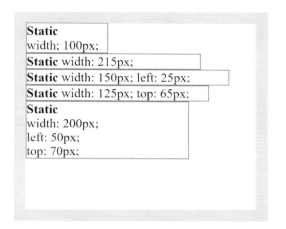
position: static;

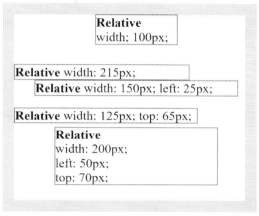
position: relative;

Figure 50: **Left:** `position:static;` **Right:** the same exact elements – the only thing that was changed was `position:relative;`

Essentially, `static` and `relative` elements are the same, except `relative` elements can have a `top` and `left` offset relative to their original location. Relative elements can also have `right` and `bottom` offsets.

Using *relative* position works well for creating offsets when working with text. Although, it is more proper to use `padding` and `margin` properties to achieve the same effect. You will find that *relative* positioning is not enough for arranging blocking elements like images, at a specific location inside the area of a parent element.

Hence, `position:relative;` should not be relied upon for complete precision, when you need an element to be placed at a pixel-perfect location within its parent container. For that purpose, `position:absolute;` should be used.

5.3 absolute & fixed

Figure 51: `absolute` is used for pixel-perfect placement inside a parent container. The `fixed` elements are almost identical to `absolute`. Except they don't respond to changes in scrollbar position.

Above is an example of how `absolute` and `fixed` elements *collapse* parent element if no dimensions are supplied to the parent container. This might sound like an unimportant detail, but you will often find yourself running into these cases every now and then *while* designing layouts, especially when switching your elements from `relative` to `absolute` placement.

Throughout this chapter, we'll take a look at more practical examples.

Note that if parent's `width` and `height` are not explicitly specified, applying `absolute` (or `fixed`) to its only child will collapse its dimensions to 0 x 0, but the child will still be positioned relative to it.

Figure 52: **Left:** Absolutely positioned elements do not populate their parent container with content. They sort of float above them, while still retaining position relative to their container element. **Right:** Here, the parent's element's dimensions were explicitly set. Technically, there is no effect on child with position:absolute, its pivot point is still located at 0 x 0 of the parent.

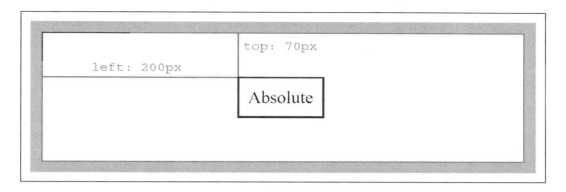

Figure 53: In order for elements using `position:absolute` to be aligned relative to their parent, the parent's `position` property must not be set to `static` (*default*).

It may seem that elements with `absolute` positioning float independently of the parent container. But that's not entirely true. In order to understand how `absolute` position affects the element to which it is applied, we need to draw the line between *two unique cases* you will often encounter.

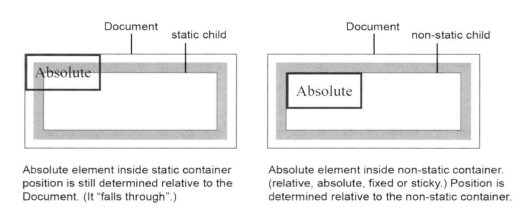

Figure 54: Elements with absolute position have different behavior based on whether they are inside a static or non-static container.

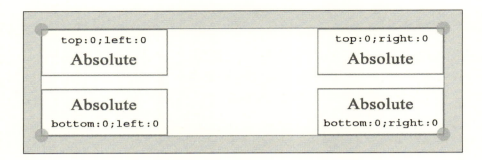

Figure 55: Using `position:absolute` to align elements at parent's corners.

You can use `top`, `left`, `bottom` and `right` in combination to change the starting point from which the offset will be calculated. You cannot use `left` and `right` at the same time. Just like you can't use `top` and `bottom` at the same time. One will override the other if used together.

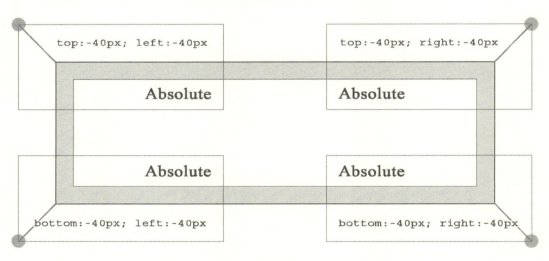

Figure 56: Using `position:absolute` with negative values.

5.4 fixed

Fixed works in exactly the same way as absolute, except that it won't respond to scrollbar. Elements will remain at the location on the screen (relative to the document) where they were placed regardless of the current scrollbar position.

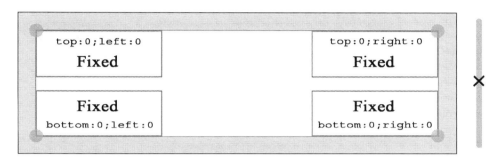

Figure 57: Using `position:fixed` to place elements to a fixed location on the screen relative to the document.

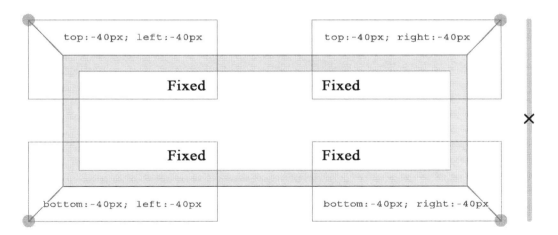

Figure 58: Using `position:fixed` with negative values.

5.5 sticky

Sticky was one of the latest additions to CSS. In the past, you would have to write custom JavaScript code or media query to achieve the same effect.

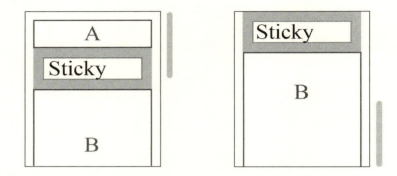

Figure 59: `sticky` is often used for creating *floating* navigation bars.

```
.navbar {
    /* Define some basic setings */
    padding: 0px;
    border: 20px solid silver;
    background-color: white;
    /* Add stickiness */
    position: -webkit-sticky;
    position: sticky;
    top: 0;
}
```

Figure 60: Simple code to make navigation bar "stick" to the upper (`top:0`) border of the screen. Note that `-webkit-sticky` was added here also for compatibility with webkit-based browsers (*such as Chrome*).

6 Working With Text

We will not spend much space on diagrams for text because you have virtually seen that everywhere by just browsing websites or using social media websites. The primary properties for changing text in CSS are `font-family`, `font-size`, `color`, `font-weight` (*normal* or *bold*), `font-style` (*italic*, for example) and `text-decoration` (*underline* or *none*).

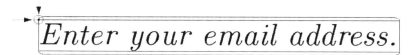

Figure 61: font-family:"CMU Classical Serif"; is the font used in the creation of this book. I suggest you check it out because it's one of the very best fonts around.

Figure 62: font-family: "CMU Bright"; is a variation of the CMU family fonts. Another nice-looking font!

Figure 63: font-family: Arial, sans-serif; is Google's favorite.

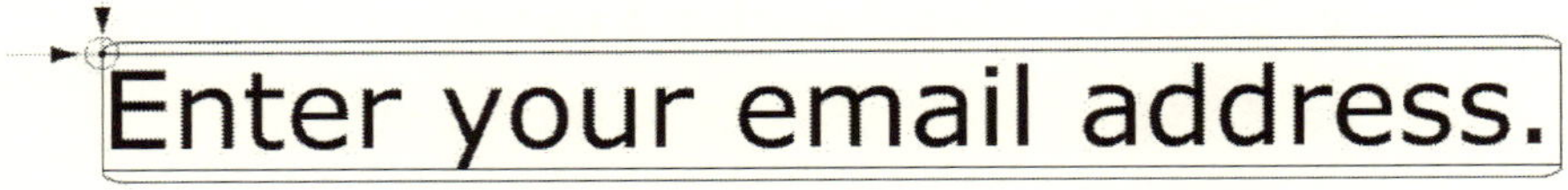

Enter your email address.

Figure 64: font-family: Verdana, sans-serif.

Note the sans-serif font is used here as a fall back font. You can specify even more fonts, separating them by comma. If the first font on the list is not available or cannot be rendered by current browser, CSS will fall back to the next available font on the list. Times New Roman, shown in the last example here will be used if no other font was found.

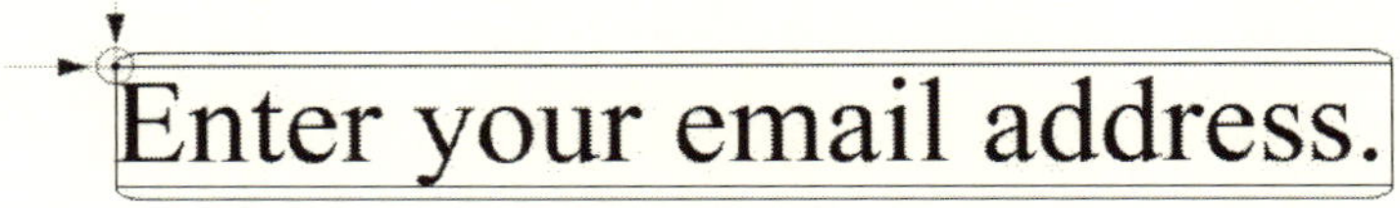

Enter your email address.

Figure 65: Times New Roman. The default browser font.

Enter your email address.
Arial 12px
Enter your email address
Arial 16px
Enter your email address
Arial 20px

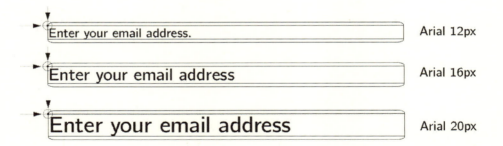

Figure 66: You can change the size of your font with `font-size` property. `16px` is the default "medium" size.

pt	px	em	%	size	default sans-serif
6pt	8px	0.5em	50%		Sample text
7pt	9px	0.55em	55%		Sample text
7.5pt	10px	0.625em	62.5%	x-small	Sample text
8pt	11px	0.7em	70%		Sample text
9pt	12px	0.75em	75%		Sample text
10pt	13px	0.8em	80%	small	Sample text
10.5pt	14px	0.875em	87.5%		Sample text
11pt	15px	0.95em	95%		Sample text
12pt	16px	1em	100%	medium	Sample text
13pt	17px	1.05em	105%		Sample text
13.5pt	18px	1.125em	112.5%	large	Sample text
14pt	19px	1.2em	120%		Sample text
14.5pt	20px	1.25em	125%		Sample text
15pt	21px	1.3em	130%		Sample text
16pt	22px	1.4em	140%		Sample text
17pt	23px	1.45em	145%		Sample text
18pt	24px	1.5em	150%	x-large	Sample text
20pt	26px	1.6em	160%		Sample text
22pt	29px	1.8em	180%		Sample text
24pt	32px	2em	200%	xx-large	Sample text
26pt	35px	2.2em	220%		Sample text
27pt	36px	2.25em	225%		Sample text
28pt	37px	2.3em	230%		Sample text
29pt	38px	2.35em	235%		Sample text
30pt	40px	2.45em	245%		Sample text
32pt	42px	2.55em	255%		Sample text
34pt	45px	2.75em	275%		Sample text
36pt	48px	3em	300%		Sample text

Figure 67: Font size can be specified using pt, px, em or % units. By default 100% is the same as 12pt, 16px or 1em. Knowing this you can extrapolate values to arrive at either a bigger or smaller font relative to the default size.

font-weight	Raleway
100	Thin
200	Extra-Light
300	Light
400	Regular
500	Medium
600	Semi-Bold
700	Bold
800	Extra-Bold
900	Black

Figure 68: `font-weight` is demonstrated here on custom *Raleway* font available via Google Fonts.

6.1 Text Align

Aligning text within an HTML element is one of the most basic things you can do in CSS.

Figure 69: `text-align: left;` is the default.

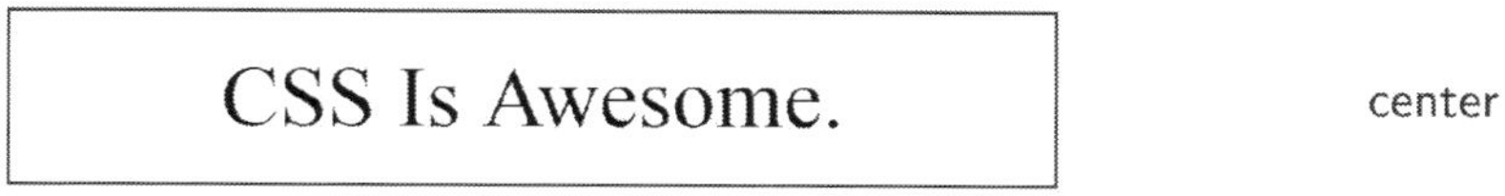

Figure 70: `text-align: center;`

Figure 71: `text-align: right;`

6.2 Text Align Last

The `text-align-last` is the same as `text-align` except it refers only to the very last line of text in a paragraph:

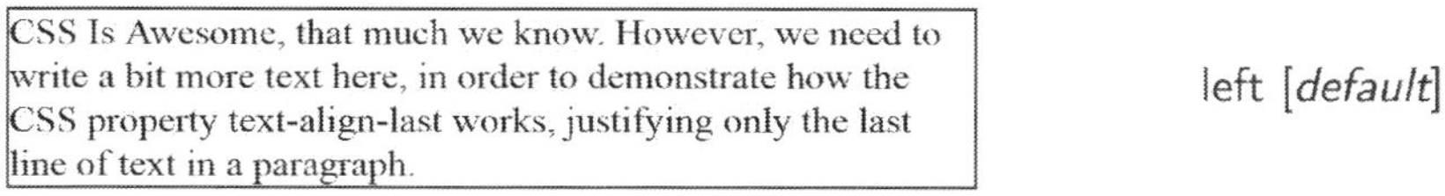

Figure 72: `text-align-last: left;`

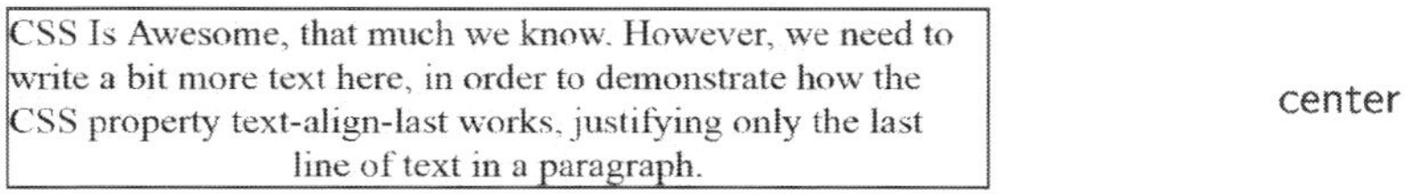

Figure 73: `text-align-last:center;`

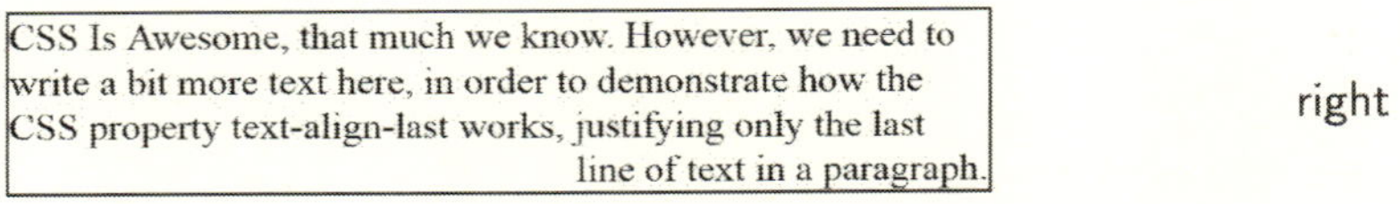

CSS Is Awesome, that much we know. However, we need to write a bit more text here, in order to demonstrate how the CSS property text-align-last works, justifying only the last line of text in a paragraph.

right

Figure 74: `text-align-last:right;`

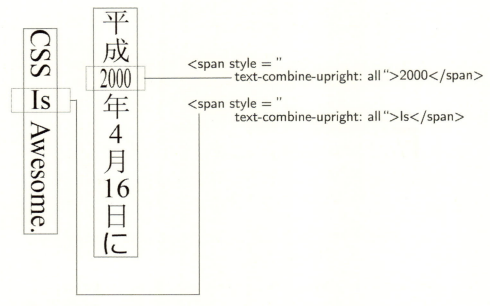

writing-mode: vertical-lr;

Figure 75: When `writing-mode` is set to `vertical`, you can also use `text-combine-upright: all` to produce the scenario shown on this diagram.

6.3 Overflow

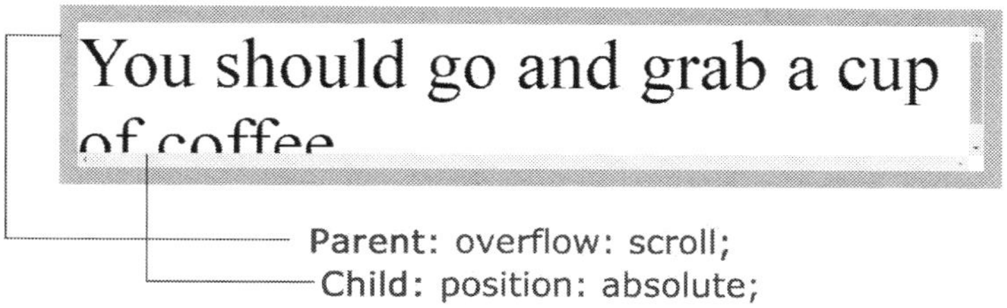

Figure 76: When text is nested within a parent element you can make it scrollable by applying `overflow:scroll` to the parent.

Figure 77: `overflow auto; height:24px;`

Figure 78: `overflow:auto; height:34px;`

> You should go and grab a cup of coffee.
>
> Parent: overflow: hidden
> Child: position: absolute;

Figure 79: `overflow:hidden;` and `position:absolute;`

overflow: hidden;

Figure 80: The classic case of `overflow:hidden;` You should go and grab a cup of coffee.

CSS Is Awesome.	overline
CSS Is Awesome.	line-through
CSS Is Awesome.	underline
CSS Is Awesome.	underline overline
CSS Is Awesome.	underline overline dotted red
CSS Is Awesome.	underline overline wavy blue
CSS Is Awesome.	underline overline double green

Figure 81: Note separate values are separated by space. You'll see a lot of this across the whole spectrum of CSS value combinations usually used as "shorthands" for individual properties. You can add underline to text using `text-decoration` property on both top and bottom of the text. Though this property is uncommon in layout design, it's nice to know it exists and is supported by all browsers.

6.4 Skip Ink

The `text-decoration-skip-ink` property can be used to superimpose text over the underline. This is actually useful for improving visual integrity of page titles or any underlined text that must use large letters.

You should go and grab a cup of coffee.

text-decoration: underline solid blue
text-decoration-skip-ink: none

You should go and grab a cup of coffee.

text-decoration: underline solid blue
text-decoration-skip-ink: auto

6.5 Text Rendering

The `text-rendering` property will probably not produce a noticeable difference in the four of its manifestations (`auto`, `optimizeSpeed`, `optimizeLegibility` and `geometricPrecision`). But it is believed that in some browsers using `optimizeSpeed` value is known to improve rendering speed of large blocks of text. The `optimizeLegibility` is the only value that actually produced a physical difference on the text in our experiments with Chrome browser, by shifting words closer together in some character combinations.

CSS Is Awesome.

text-rendering: auto;

CSS Is Awesome.

text-rendering: optimizeSpeed;

text-rendering: optimizeLegibility;

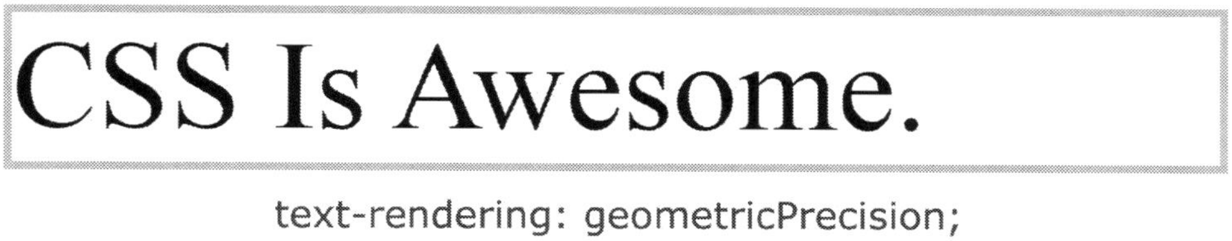

CSS Is Awesome.

text-rendering: geometricPrecision;

The names of the four possible values used here are self-explanatory to their intended function.

6.6 Text Indent

The text-indent property will take care of aligning your text. It is rarely used but in some cases, specifically, news sites for example, or book editing software, they might prove to be useful.

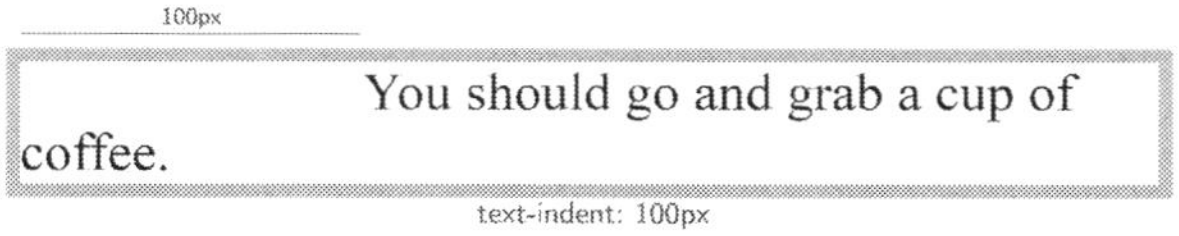

Figure 82: `text-indent:100px;`

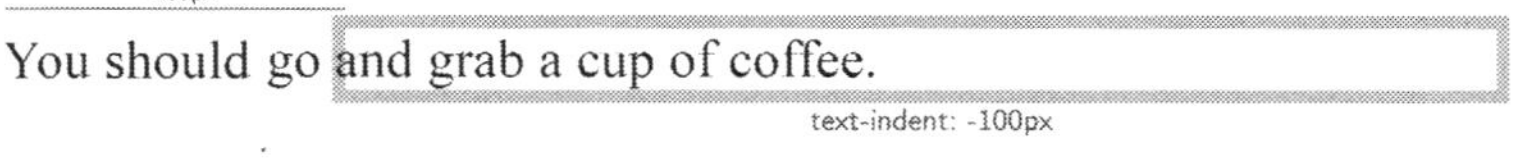

Figure 83: `text-indent:-100px;`

6.7 Text Orientation

Text orientation is controlled by `text-orientation` property. Might be useful for rendering text in different languages where the flow of text can either go from right to left or from top down. Often used together with `writing-mode` property.

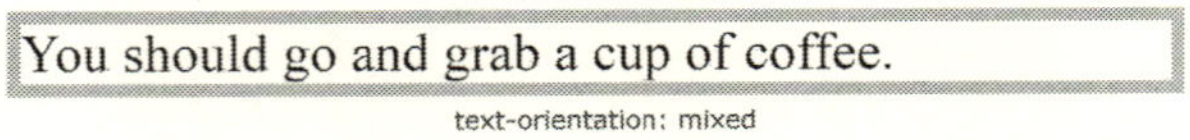
You should go and grab a cup of coffee.
text-orientation: mixed

Figure 84: `text-orientation:upright;`

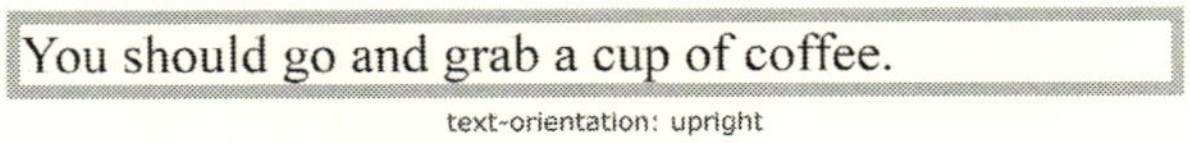
You should go and grab a cup of coffee.
text-orientation: upright

Figure 85: `text-orientation:upright;`

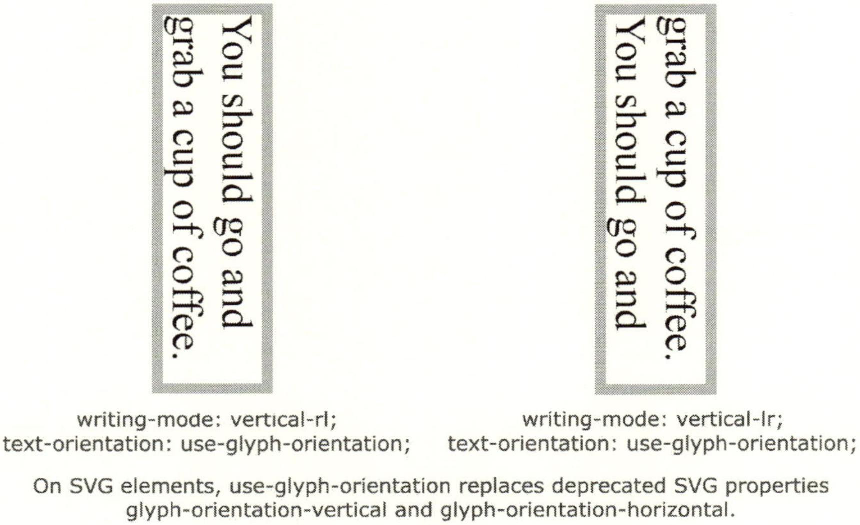
You should go and
grab a cup of coffee.
grab a cup of coffee.
You should go and
writing-mode: vertical-rl;
text-orientation: use-glyph-orientation;
writing-mode: vertical-lr;
text-orientation: use-glyph-orientation;
On SVG elements, use-glyph-orientation replaces deprecated SVG properties
glyph-orientation-vertical and glyph-orientation-horizontal.

Figure 86: Together with `writing-mode:vertical-rl` (right to left) or `writing-mode:vertical-lr` (left to right) the `text-orientation` property can be used to produce text align in pretty much any direction.

The same as before only this time with `text-orientation` set to `upright`:

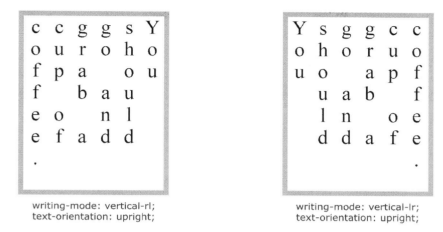

Figure 87: `text-orientation:upright; writing-mode:vertical-rl;`

Figure 88: To center text vertically in any element set its line height with `line-height:60px;` to the height of the element. Text size (the height of actual letters) and its `line-height` are not always the same.

Figure 89: Ligatures with `font-feature-settings: "liga" 1`, or alternatively `font-feature-settings: "liga" on`

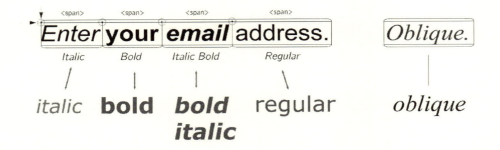

Figure 90: Common text effects (*italic*, *bold*, and *oblique*) are achieved by using the properties `font-style` and `font-weight`.

Figure 91: The `text-align` and `line-height` properties are often used to center text inside buttons.

6.8 Text Shadow

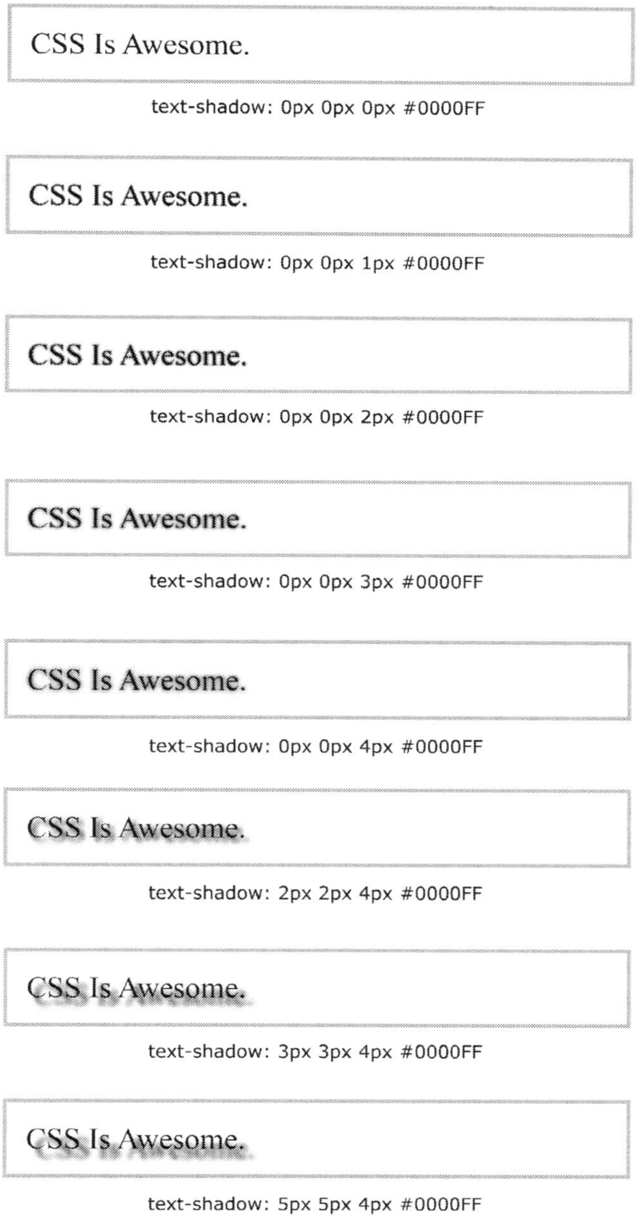

CSS Is Awesome.

text-shadow: 0px 0px 0px #0000FF

CSS Is Awesome.

text-shadow: 0px 0px 1px #0000FF

CSS Is Awesome.

text-shadow: 0px 0px 2px #0000FF

CSS Is Awesome.

text-shadow: 0px 0px 3px #0000FF

CSS Is Awesome.

text-shadow: 0px 0px 4px #0000FF

CSS Is Awesome.

text-shadow: 2px 2px 4px #0000FF

CSS Is Awesome.

text-shadow: 3px 3px 4px #0000FF

CSS Is Awesome.

text-shadow: 5px 5px 4px #0000FF

Figure 92: You can add a shadow to your text using `text-shadow` property. See the next diagram to understand its parameters.

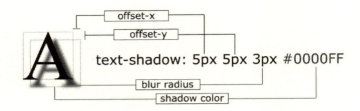

Figure 93: The `text-shadow` property takes the offset on both x and y axis, *blur radius* and *shadow color*.

We won't be going much into SVG, which can also be controlled by CSS properties. An entire book can be written on the subject alone. But as a brief inset here, you can create rotated SVG text as follows:

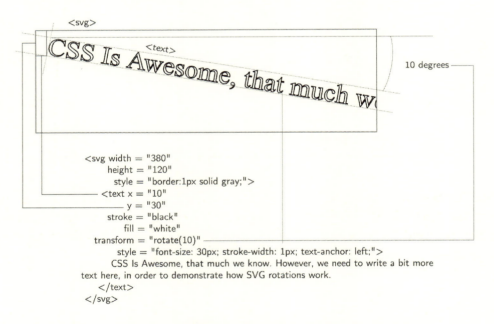

Figure 94: Using CSS to manipulate SVG text rotation.

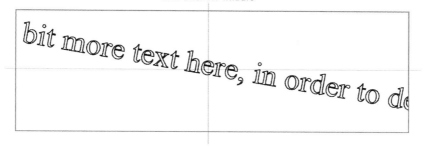

Figure 95: Using `text-anchor` it's possible to set the center point of the text, around which it will be rotated.

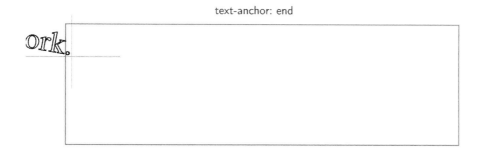

Figure 96: Setting `text-anchor` to `end` to offset center of rotation to the very end of the text block. We'll see similar behavior on CSS transform property that can be used to rotate entire HTML elements and text within them.

7 Margin, Rounded Corners, Box Shadow and Z-Index

These few subjects, in no particular order, were chosen to briefly demonstrate commonly used CSS properties.

7.1 Border Radius

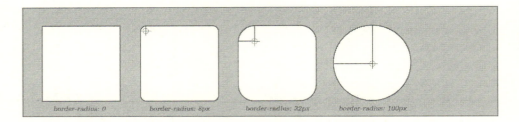

Figure 97: The `border-radius` is the property used to add rounded corners to square or rectangular HTML elements.

Figure 98: Using the `:hover` *pseudo-selector* you can choose what happens when the mouse hovers (enters the area of) over an element.

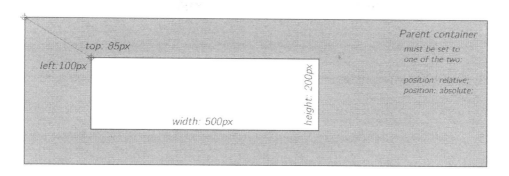

Figure 99: The parent container **must** be explicitly set to either `position:relative` or `position:absolute` in order to use a child element within it that also uses `position:absolute` align.

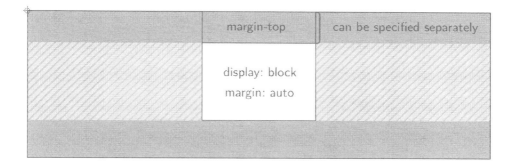

Figure 100: You can use `margin:auto` to align an element horizontally. Just make sure its `display` property is set to `block`; The property `margin-top` can be used to offset an element by a space on its upper side. You can also use `margin-left`, `margin-right`, `margin-bottom`.

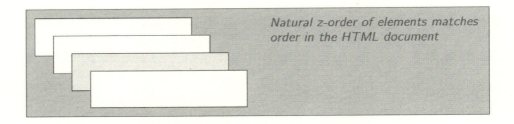

Figure 101: The `z-index` property takes a *numeric value* between **0 - 2147483647** to determine element's drawing order on most common browsers. In Safari 3 the maximum `z-index` value is **16777271**.

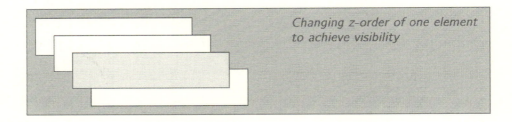

Figure 102: Changing `z-order` of one element to change visibility order and make it stand out.

Figure 103: Here `box-shadow` is used to add a shadow around a wide element. It takes the same parameters `text-shadow` does, for example: `box-shadow: 5px 5px 10px #000` (x and y offset, *radius* of the shadow, and shadow *color*.)

Figure 104: The property `box-radius` controls the radius of the corner's curve on both X and Y axis.

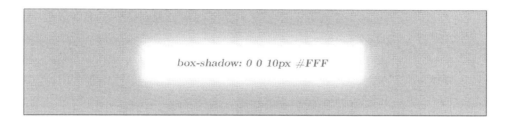

Figure 105: Using bright colors with `box-shadow` property it is possible to create glowing effect around HTML elements.

Figure 106: Just what you would expect from a simple blocking element.

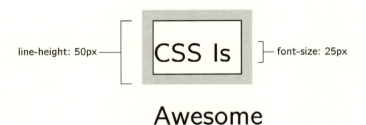

Figure 107: When the width of an element becomes smaller than the width of its text content, text automatically moves to the next available line, even if it exists outside of the element's boundary.

Let's take an even closer look at the previous scenarios.

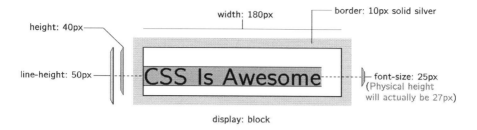

Figure 108: The physical height of the text will actually be 27px, 2 pixels more than 25px – the original value set. The value provided by line-height can stretch outside of content area.

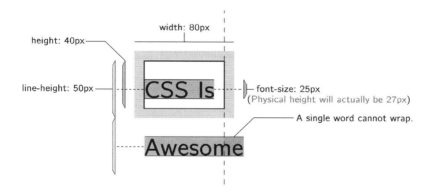

Figure 109: Here we can clearly see that the word "Awesome" jumped over to the next line. In addition to this, note that a single word cannot wrap around the container element even if its width is smaller. In other words, overflow property is visible by *default*.

You can effectively cut off the content outside of the content container by setting `overflow:hidden`. This will work even on elements with rounded corners:

Figure 110: `overflow:hidden` works on rounded corners.

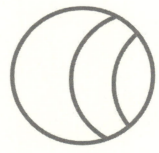

Figure 111: Hiding other round elements within a circle can create some interesting, irregular shapes.

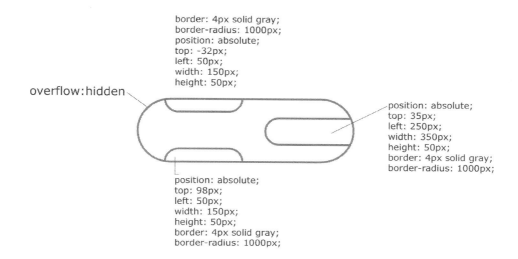

Figure 112: By using multiple elements with `overflow:hidden` it is possible to create irregular shapes.

Figure 113: The same as previous example, except with parent container `background` set to `gray`, and the `background` of elements within it set to `white`. You can get really creative with this and make some interesting objects. We'll take a look at an entire car example toward the end of the book.

8 Nike Logo

By combining techniques from previous section with `transform:rotate` (*it will be discussed in greater detail later in the book*) and our current knowledge of `:before` and `:after` pseudo selectors, it is possible to create the NIKE logo from a single HTML element:

Figure 114: Nike logo created 1 HTML element and 3 CSS commands.

Let's define our main container:

```
 1  #nike {
 2      position: absolute;
 3      top: 300px; left: 300px;
 4      width: 470px; height: 200px;
 5      border: 1px solid gray;
 6      overflow: hidden;
 7      font-family: Arial, sans-serif;
 8      font-size: 40px;
 9      line-height: 300px;
10      text-indent: 350px;
11      z-index: 3;
12  }
```

Note `overflow:hidden` here is used to ensure everything outside of the container is clipped away.

Using `#nike:before` and `#nike:after` pseudo elements we'll create the base of the logo which is a long black bar. Rounded corners used here to create the famous Nike curve:

```css
#nike:before {
    content: "";
    position: absolute;
    top: -250px;
    left: 190px;
    width: 150px;
    height: 550px;
    background: black;
    border-top-left-radius: 60px 110px;
    border-top-right-radius: 130px 220px;
    transform: rotate(-113deg);
    z-index: 1;
}
```

Similarly, we'll create another curved box. Its white background will serve as a mask to block out the rest of the logo. Here, the rotation angle is everything. It's what forms the recognizable curve of the logo. We've also used `z-index` of 1, 2 and 3 respectively to ensure proper layering of the elements.

```css
#nike:after {
    content: "";
    position: absolute;
    top: -235px;
    left: 220px;
    width: 120px;
    height: 500px;
    background: black;
    border-top-left-radius: 60px 110px;
    border-top-right-radius: 130px 220px;
    background: white;
    transform: rotate(-104deg);
    z-index: 2;
}
```

Here is another view of the logo. This time with transparent background, so we can actually its geometric composition:

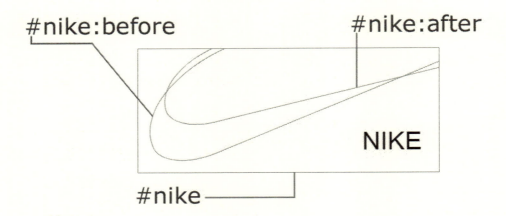

Figure 115: Composition of the Nike logo, consisting of 3 elements (1 HTML element and its 2 pseudo-element counterparts.)

The actual HTML is just one **div** element with **id** nike.

```
1    <div id = "nike">NIKE</div>
```

9 Display

CSS properties are used to assign behavior to HTML elements that determine their placement on the screen. Diagrams in this section demonstrate the effect on each element in a set of common cases.

The CSS property `display` can take any one of the several values: `inline`, `block`, `inline-block` or `float` to define placement of individual elements.

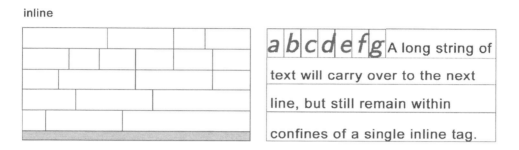

Figure 116: `display:inline`. This is the `default` value used for `<span>`, `<b>`, `<i>` and a few other HTML tags created for dealing with displaying text inside parent containers with unknown width.

Here, each element is placed directly on the right hand side after the length of its content (or its width) in the previous element has been exceeded, making it the natural option for displaying text.

Note: *long* inline elements are automatically carried over to the next row.

Later, when we arrive at the Flex and CSS grid chapters, you will see how applying the values `flex` or `grid` to the `display` property can modify the behavior of its *items* – elements residing inside a container element, often referred to as their *parent* element.

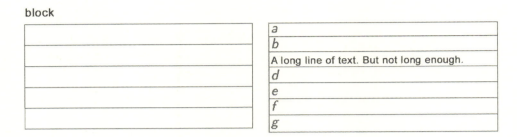

Figure 117: `display:block` – in contrast to `inline` elements – will automatically block an entire row of space, regardless of the width of its content. The HTML tags `<div>` is a blocking element by default.

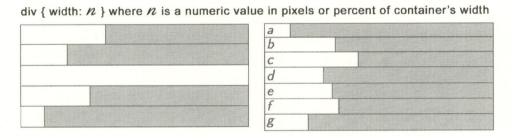

Figure 118: `display:block`, with explicitly defined element widths introduces the idea of discerning between element's container width and its content width.

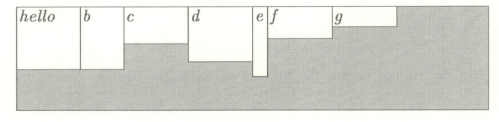

Figure 119: `display:inline-block` *combines* `inline` and `blocking` behavior to enable custom size for inline elements

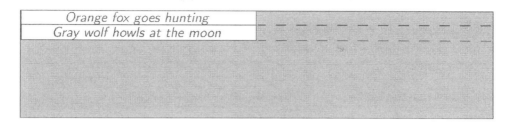

Figure 120: Centered text (`text-align:center`) inside two blocking elements with width set to 50% of the container. Note, that while blocking the entire row of the parent element, the content area only stretches up to 50% of its width. A blocking element is not defined by the width of its content.

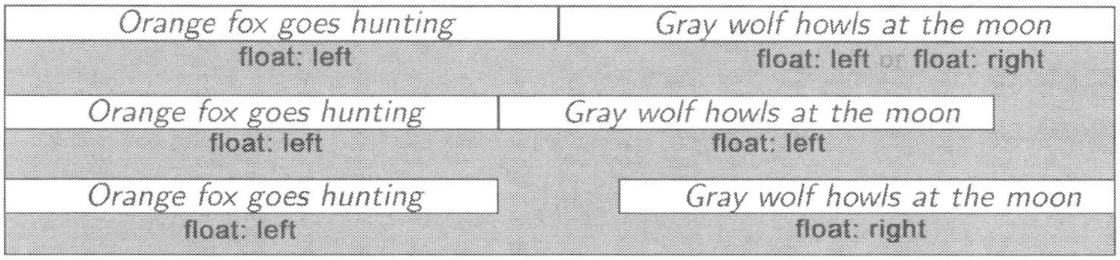

Figure 121: Two blocking elements with explicit width of about 50% and `text-align:center` can somewhat imitate inline elements by also applying `float:left` and/or `float:right`. However, unlike inline elements, a single blocking element can never cross over to the next row.

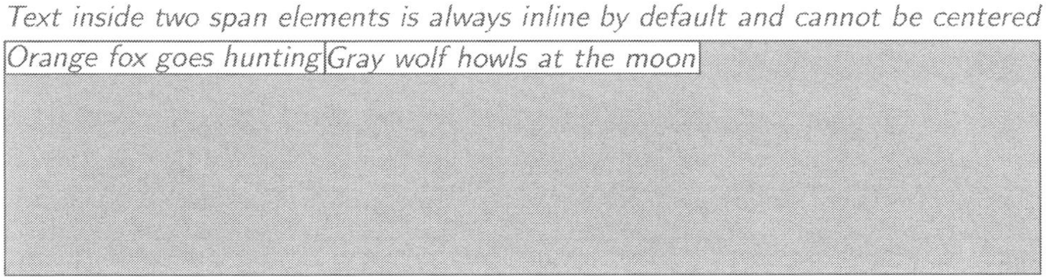

Figure 122: Inline elements are always limited to the width of their content and therefore text within them cannot be centered.

10   Element Visibility

Element's visibility can hide the element's box without completely removing it from the drawing hierarchy.

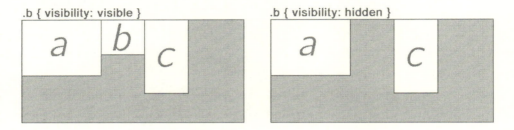

Figure 123: Setting `visibility` property to `hidden` on "b" element. The default is `visible` (Same as `unset`, or `auto`, or `none`).

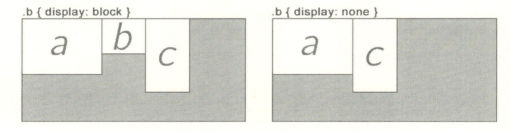

Figure 124: `display:none` completely removes the element.

11 Floating Elements

Figure 125: Blocking elements with `float:left` and `float:right` appear on the same row, as long as the sum of their widths is less than the width of the parent element.

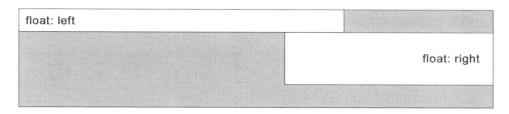

Figure 126: If the total sum of two floating element's is greater than parent's width, one of them will be blocked by the other and skip over to the next row.

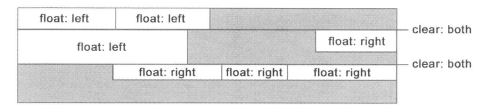

Figure 127: You can use `clear:both` to clear floating elements and start a new floating row.

12 Color Gradients

Gradients can be used for a variety of reasons. But the most common thing they're usually used for is to provide a smooth shading effect across the area of some User Interface element.

Here are a couple more reasons for using them:

Smooth Background Color Shading provides an elegant solution for making your HTML elements more appealing to the eye.

Saving Bandwidth is another benefit of using gradients, because they are automatically generated in browser by an efficient color shading algorithm. This means that they can be used instead of images, which would otherwise take a lot longer to download from the web server.

Simple Definitions can be used in `background` property to create some quite interesting and sometimes surprising effects. You will be supplying the minimum required parameters to either `linear-gradient` or `radial-gradient` properties to create any of the effects demonstrated in the next section.

12.1 Overview

In this chapter we will learn how to create these gradients in HTML:

Figure 128: If this is a black and white print, you will not see the difference between gradients that actually use color. However, to master gradients you really only need a good grasp on their direction and type of which there are four – `linear-gradient`, `radial-gradient`, `repeating-linear-gradient` and `repeating-radial-gradient`. This diagram gives you a good idea of the variety of gradients it is possible to create for your HTML elements with CSS.

I cheated a little here... the images above are files from my gradients folder that I created while working on this book. But how do we actually create them using CSS commands? The rest of this chapter will provide a solution!

Specimen Element for Displaying Gradients

We will perform our experiments with the background gradients using this simple DIV element. Let's set some basic properties to it first, including width=500px and height=500px.

For now, we just need a simple square element. Paste this code anywhere in between `<head>` tags in your HTML document.

```
1  <style type = "text/css">
2  div {
```

```
3    position: relative;
4    display: block;
5    width: 500px;
6    height: 500px;
7  }
8  <style>
```

This CSS code will turn every `<div>` element on the screen to a square with dimensions of 500 by 500 pixels. The `position` and `display` properties will be explained further in the book.

Alternatively, we probably want to assign gradients only to one HTML element. In which case you can either specify the CSS to an individual `div` element using a unique ID such as `#my-gradient-box` *or any other that makes sense to you.*

```
1  <style type="text/css">
2  div#my-gradient-box { position: relative; display: block;
       width: 500px; height: 500px; }
3  <style>
```

And then add it somewhere within your `<body>` tag as:

```
1  <!-- Experimenting with Color Gradient Backgrounds in HTML
       //-->
2  <div id="my-gradient-box"></div>
```

Or type the same CSS commands directly into `style` attribute of an HTML element you wish to apply a color gradient to:

```
1  <div style="position: relative; display: block; width: 500
       px; height: 500px;"></div>
```

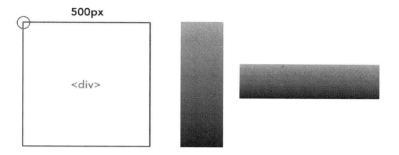

Figure 129: A div element with dimension of 500 x 500 pixels. The row and column on the right hand side demonstrate how gradients automatically adapt to the element's size. The gradient property was not changed here. Only the element's dimensions, yet the gradient looks quite different. Keep this in mind when making your own gradients!

CSS gradients will automatically adapt to the element's width and height. *Which might produce a slightly different effect.*

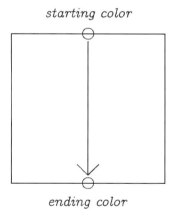

Figure 130: The basic idea behind gradients is to interpolate between at least two colors. By default, without providing any extra values, vertical direction is assumed. The starting color will begin at the top of the element, gradually blending in with 100% of the second color at the bottom. It's possible to create gradients by combining more than two colors. We'll take a look at that in a moment!

All CSS gradient values are supplied to CSS `background` property!

Having said that, here's an example of creating a simple linear gradient:

```
1   background: linear-gradient(black, white);
```

These values will be demonstrated in action below, shown just underneath the gradient effect they produce.

12.2 Gradient Types

Let's walk through different gradient styles one by one and visualize the type of gradient effects you would expect to be rendered within the HTML element, when these styles are applied to it.

linear-gradient(black, white)   *linear-gradient(yellow, red)*

Figure 131: A simple linear gradient. Left: black to white. Right: yellow to red.

Figure 132: Horizontal gradients can be created by specifying a leading value of either "to left" or "to right", depending on which direction you wish your gradient to flow across the element.

Figure 133: You can start gradients at corners too to create diagonal color transitions. Values "to top left", "to top right", "to bottom left" and "to bottom right" can be used to achieve that effect.

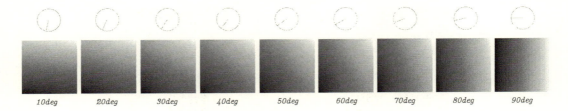

Figure 134: When 45 degree corners are not enough, you can supply a custom degree between 0 – 360 directly to the `linear-gradient` property as in `linear-gradient(30deg, black, white);` Notice how in this example the gradient gradually changes direction from flowing toward the bottom, toward the left hand side when angle is changed in progression from 10 to 90 degrees.

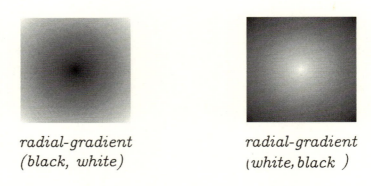

Figure 135: Radial gradients can be created by using `radial-gradient` property. Swapping colors around will produce an inverse effect.

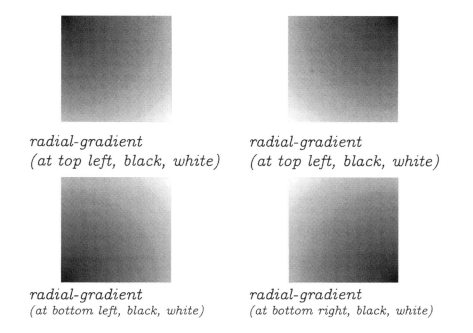

Figure 136: In the same way as linear gradients, radial gradients can also take origin at any of the four corners of an HTML element.

 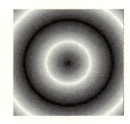

repeating-linear-gradient (white 100px, black 200px, white 300px);

repeating-radial-gradient (white 100px, black 200px, white 300px);

Figure 137: Repetitive patterns for linear and radial gradients can be created using `repeating-linear-gradient` and `repeating-radial-gradient` respectively. You can provide as many repetitive color values in a row as needed. Just don't forget to separate them by a comma!

linear-gradient
   hsl(0,100%,50%),
   hsl(50,100%,50%),
   hsl(100,100%,50%),
   hsl(150,100%,50%),
   hsl(200,100%,50%),
   hsl(250,100%,50%),
   hsl(300,100%,50%)

linear-gradient
   hsl(0,100%,50%),
   hsl(50,100%,50%),
   hsl(300,100%,50%)

Figure 138: Finally – the most advanced type of a gradient can be created using a series of HSL values. HSL values don't have named or RGB equivalents, they are counted on a scale from 0 – 300. See the explanation below.

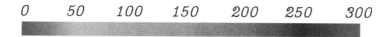

Figure 139: You can cherry-pick any color by using values between 0 – 300.

We've already provided examples of property values associated with each gradient. But here they are again in one place. Play around with the values and see what type of effects they produce on your custom UI elements:

```
1  background: linear-gradient(yellow, red);
2  background: linear-gradient(black, white);
3  background: linear-gradient(to right, black, white);
4  background: linear-gradient(to left, black, white);
5  background: linear-gradient(to bottom right, black, white);
6  background: linear-gradient(90deg, black, white);
7  background: linear-gradient(
8  hsl(0,100%,50%),
9  hsl(50,100%,50%),
10 hsl(100,100%,50%),
11 hsl(150,100%,50%),
12 hsl(200,100%,50%),
13 hsl(250,100%,50%),
14 hsl(300,100%,50%));
15 background: radial-gradient(black, white);
16 background: radial-gradient(at bottom right, black, white);
17 background:
18 repeating-linear-gradient
19 (white 100px, black 200px, white 300px);
20 background:
21 repeating-radial-gradient
22 (white 100px, black 200px, white 300px);
```

13 Filters

CSS filters modify appearance of an image (*or any HTML element that has graphics output of some sorts*) by adjusting its color values. Filters are applied using `filter` property that takes a function with a single argument.

The value of filter functions like *__blur__*, *__contrast__*, *__brightness__*, etc. can be specified in *__percent__*, as a *__number__* or pixel value (*__px__*).

13.1 blur()

Perhaps the most useful of all CSS filters is the blur effect.

```
001 .blur { filter: blur(100px); }
```

filter: blur(0);   filter: blur(100px);

Figure 140: The blur filter with strength of `100px` applied to a bird image.

The blur filter is quite versatile in that it can work together with images that contain transparent areas, creating many opportunities for making interesting visual effects and UI transitions.

Unfortunately, most of the other CSS filters don't have much practical use (*For example, have you ever seen a sepia photo filter on any websites?*) but they are still included here to be complete.

13.2 brightness()

```
001 .blur { filter: blur(100px); }
```

Adjust brightness of the HTML element (*or an image*). Values are provided in floating point format `0.0 - 1.0`, where `1.0` equals the original image content. Greater values than `1.0` are allowed. They will simply make your image brighter than its original pixel values.

13.3 contrast()

Change contrast of the image / HTML element. The level of contrast is specified in percentage.

```
001 .contrast { filter: contrast(120%); }
```

13.4 grayscale()

Desaturate colors by percent value.

```
001 .grayscale { filter: grayscale(100%); }
```

13.5 hue-rotate()

Change color hue. Value is provided in degrees (`0deg - 360deg`).

```
001 .hue-rotate { filter: hue-rotate(180deg); }
```

13.6 invert()

Invert colors. Value is provided in percent. Value of 50% creates a gray image.

```
001 .invert { filter: invert(100%); }
```

13.7 opacity()

Modify element opacity (similar to `opacity` property.)

```
001 .opacity { filter: opacity(50%); }
```

13.8 saturate()

Saturate colors: value is provided as a number between 0 - 100. Values greater than 100 are also possible, which usually result in an overly-saturated image.

```
001 .saturate { filter: saturate(7); }
```

13.9 sepia()

Apply sepia tone effect (*Looks like an aged photograph.*)

```
001 .sepia { filter: sepia(100%); }
```

13.10 drop-shadow()

```
001 .shadow { filter: drop-shadow(8px 8px 10px green); }
```

Similar to `box-shadow` property.

14 Background Images

So you think you know HTML backgrounds? Well maybe you do and maybe you don't. This section was created as a brief backgrounds tutorial that hopefully introduces the reader to the big picture. We'll explore several CSS properties that help us change background image settings on any HTML element.

Figure 141: `background: url("image.jpg")` or `background-image: url("image.jpg")`

The specimen image used in this section is this adorable kitten on a stripey background.

If the element's dimensions are bigger than those of the source image, the image will be repeated within the body of that element – repetitively filling the remainder of the element's sides with the contents of the image. It's almost like stretching infinite wallpaper across entire area of the element.

Figure 142: If the image is smaller than the element's dimensions, it will continue to repeat to fill up the remaining space.

To set the background image to any element you can use the following CSS commands.

```
1  background: url("kitten.jpg");
```

Or alternatively...

```
1  background-image: url("kitten.jpg");
```

You can also use internal CSS by placing this CSS code between `<style></style>` tags.

Let's take a look at the same kitten background... except this time around with `no-repeat` value set with the additional `background-repeat` property:

Figure 143: `background-repeat: no-repeat;`

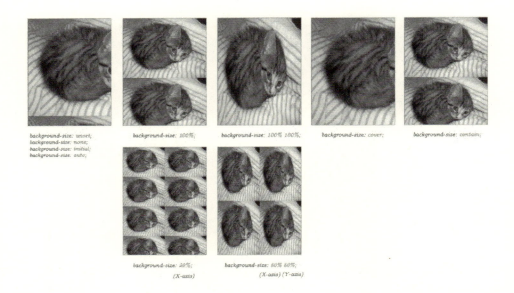

Figure 144: A closer look at the results created with `background-size`. From left to right examples are listed as follows: (*unset—none—initial—auto*) which all produce default behavior. The value of `100%` will stretch the images in horizontal direction, but not vertically. The value of `100% 100%` will stretch the image across all available space. The value `cover` will stretch the image across entire vertical space of the element, it will cut off everything in the horizontal direction, similar to overflow. The value `contain` will make sure that the image is stretched horizontally across the width of the element, and while remaining original proportion, stretch it vertically for however long it needs to, repeating the image until it overflows at the bottom of the element.

Figure 145: By combining `background-repeat: no-repeat;` with `background-size: 100%` it is possible to stretch the image only horizontally, across the entire width of the element.

What if you want to repeat background vertically but keep it stretched across the width? No problem, simply remove no-repeat from previous example.

This is what you will end up with:

Figure 146: Repeat vertically.

Above: This HTML / CSS background technique is used for sites whose content stretches vertically over a long area of space. I think one of the iterations of the Blizzard site used it in the past. Sometimes you want to cut it off, and make it static. Other times you want it to go on forever vertically. This will depend on your vision of the layout.

Sometimes it is needed to stretch the image across to fit the bounding box of an element. This often comes at a price of some distortion, however. CSS will automatically stretch the image according to some automatically-calculated percentage value:

Figure 147: Needless to say, this effect will only be observed when the HTML element and the size of the image do not match.

Above: Set `background-size:100% 100%` to stretch the image.

Note here, `100% 100%` is repeated twice. The first value tells CSS to stretch the image vertically and the second `100%` does the same horizontally. You can use values between `0 { 100%` here although I do not see many cases where this would be necessary.

14.1 Specifying Multiple Values

In HTML, whenever you need to specify multiple values they are often separated by a space. Vertical coordinates (**Y-axis** or **height**) always come first. Sometimes values are separated by comma. Example? When we need to specify multiple backgrounds they are usually separated by comma and not the space character. (*As we will see from the last section in this tutorial.*)

14.2 background-position

This is `background-position: center center` at work here.

You can force the image to be always in the center but lose repetitiveness of the pattern by specifying `no-repeat` value to `background-repeat` property:

Center the image:

```
1  background-position: center center;
```

Turn repeat off:

```
1  background-repeat: no-repeat;
```

You can repeat the image across the *x-axis* only (*horizontally*) using `repeat-x`:

Figure 148: This is `repeat-x` in action.

You can easily center and repeat the image only horizontally by supplying `repeat-x` as the value for the `background-repeat` property.

To the same effect but on the *y-axis* `repeat-y` property can be used:

Figure 149: Vertical wallpaper with `repeat-y`.

Like any other CSS property you have to juggle around the values to achieve the results you want. I think we covered pretty much everything there is about backgrounds. Except one last thing...

14.3 Multiple Backgrounds

It is possible to add more than one background to the same HTML element. The process is rather simple.

Consider these images stored in two separate files:

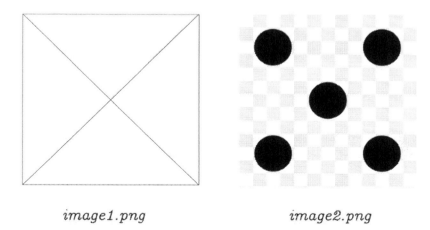

Figure 150: Finding the Magic Eraser Tool in Photoshop.

The chessboard pattern in the image on the right is only used to indicate transparency here. The white and grayish squares are not an actual part of the image itself. This is the "see-through" area which you would usually see in digital manipulation software.

When the image on the right is placed on top of other HTML elements or images, the checkered area will not block that content underneath. And this is the whole idea behind multiple backgrounds in HTML.

14.4 Image Transparency

To fully take advantage of multiple backgrounds one of the background images should have a transparent area. But how do we create one?

In this example, the second image `image2.png` contains 5 black dots on a transparent background indicated by a checkered pattern.

Like many other CSS properties that accept multiple values – all you have to do – to set up multiple backgrounds is to provide a set of values to the background property separated by comma.

14.5 Multiple Backgrounds

To assign multiple (*layered*) background images to the same HTML element, the following CSS can be used:

```
1  body { background: url("image2.png"), url("image1.png"); }
```

The order in which you supply images to the background's `url` property is important. Note that the top-most image is always listed first. This is why we start with `image2.png`.

This code produces the following result:

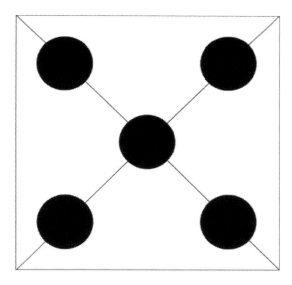

Figure 151: Superimposing a transparent image over another one using multiple backgrounds in CSS.

In this example we demonstrated multiple backgrounds in theory on a subjective `<div>` (*or similar*) element with square dimensions.

Let's take a look at another example.

puppy.png   *pattern.png*

Note here that the puppy.png image will be the first item on the comma-separated list. This is the image we want to superimpose on top of all of the other images on the list.

Combining the two:

```
1  body { background: url('puppy.png'), url('pattern.png')
```

We get the following result:

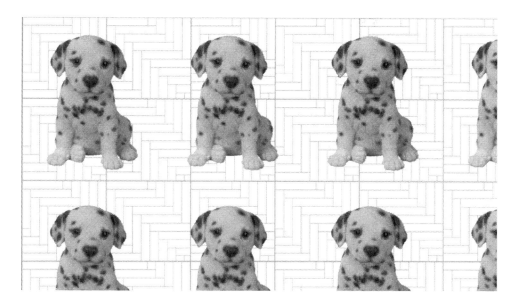

Figure 152: Background 15

Other background properties that also take comma-separated lists exist. Pretty much every other background related property other than background-color.

In the same way, you can supply other parameters to each individual background, using the other background properties demonstrated below:

```
1    background
2    background-attachment
3    background-clip
4    background-image
5    background-origin
6    background-position
7    background-repeat
8    background-size
```

The following property cannot be used with a list for obvious reasons:

```
1    background-color
```

What would it mean to provide multiple color values to a background? Whenever color background property is set, it usually fills the entire area with a solid color. But multiple backgrounds require that at least one of the backgrounds contains transparency of some sorts. Therefore, it cannot be used in the case of multiple backgrounds for any meaningful purpose.

But that's not all you can say about background images. Let's finish our discussion by taking a look at these other few cases.

14.6 background-attachment

You can determine behavior of the background image relative to scroll bar.

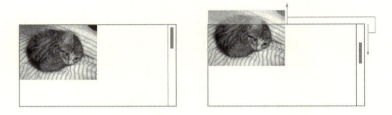

Figure 153: `background-attachment:scroll`

Before (*left*) and after (*right*) images are shown here.

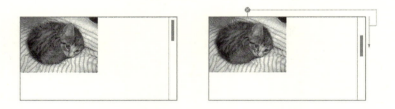

Figure 154: `background-attachment:fixed`

Fixed backgrounds don't respond to the scroll bar.

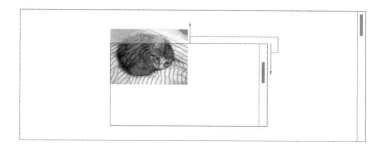

Figure 155: `background-attachment:scroll`

14.7 background-origin

Property `background-origin` determines the extent of the area that will be used by the background image, based on the *CSS Box Model*.

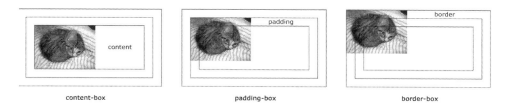

Figure 156: `content-box` — `padding-box` — `border-box`

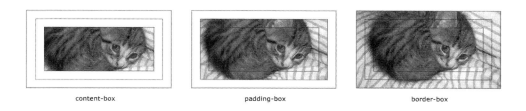

Figure 157: `content-box` — `padding-box` — `border-box`

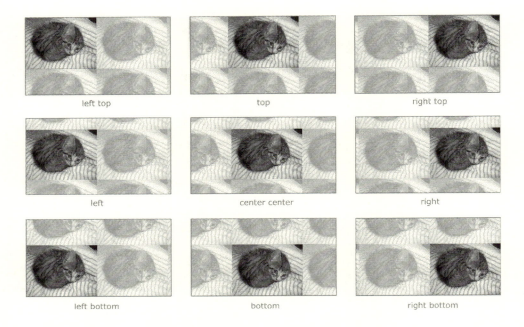

Figure 158: background-position-x and background-position-y are supplied the following values to create any of the background positioning patterns: `left top` — `top` — `right top` — `left` — `center center` — `right` — `left bottom` — `bottom` — `right bottom`.

And finally... in addition to images, the `background` property can also specify either a *solid color*, a *linear gradient* or a *radial gradient*.

Figure 159: Examples of other possible values supplied to the `background` property. Note that an entire chapter is dedicated to describing *linear* and *radial* gradients in this book.

15 object-fit

Some of the backgrounds functionality has been superseded by a slightly different image-fitting solution based on object-fit property. By providing various values you can achieve any of the following results:

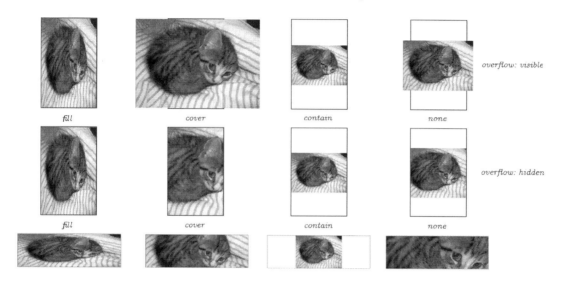

Figure 160: Here object-fit property presents us with pretty much every single possible case of how we wish to fit our object into the parent container. Note that although similar to background property, object-fit works with non-background images (created using the <img> tag), videos and other "objects", rather than background images.

The available values demonstrated in the above image examples reading from left to right are: fill, cover, contain and none.

The first row has overflow:visible. The second row has overflow:hidden. And the third row is the same as the second, but in this example the dimensions of the actual HTML element were flipped to demonstrate that it does produce a slightly different results when either vertical or horizontal dimension is prevalent over the other.

16 Borders

There is much more to CSS borders than meets the eye. In particular, you want to learn how border radius (*only when values for both X and Y axis are provided*) affects other corners of the same element. But before moving forward, let's take a look at borders.

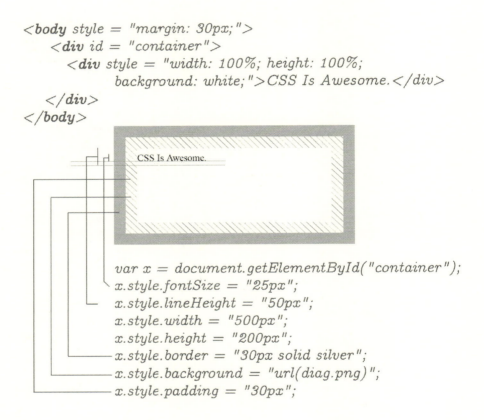

Figure 161: You can easily access all of the same CSS properties via JavaScript. Just grab an object with `document.getElementById("container")` – for example – to gain access to all CSS properties. They are attached to element.*style* property on the object.

Borders can be set on all sides at the same time with the `border` property.

```
border: 5px solid gray;
```

You can also set the curvature on each of the four corners of the element with `border-radius`, by specifying the radius of the circle:

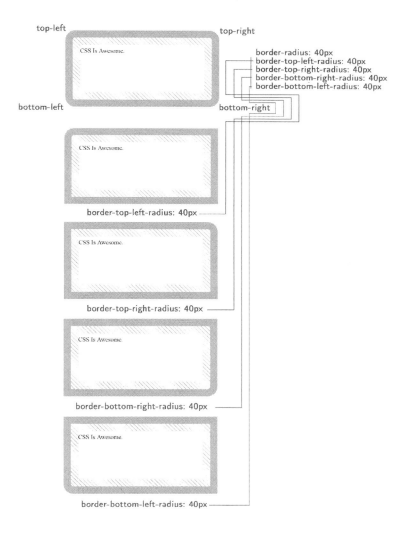

Figure 162: `border-radius`

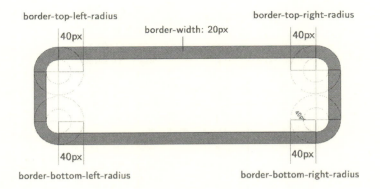

Figure 163: `border-top-left-radius` — `border-top-right-radius` — `border-bottom-left-radius` — `border-bottom-right-radius`

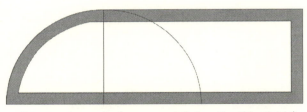

Figure 164: Using a value equal to or greater than the size of an element's side – to which border radius is applied – will be clamped to the greatest radius that fits in that area.

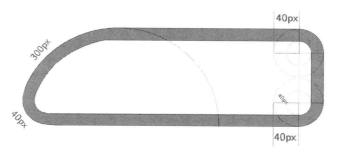

Figure 165: `border-top-left-radius:300px` — `border-top-left-radius:40px` — `border-bottom-left-radius:40px` — `border-bottom-right-radius:40px`

16.1 Elliptical Border Radius

Even after a long time working with CSS I still failed to notice that `border-radius` property can be used to create elliptical borders. But indeed, this is true. The results of elliptical curves are not always as easily predictable as is the case with axis-uniform radius values.

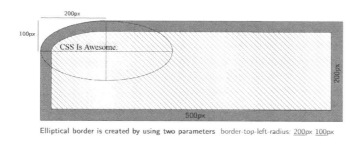

Figure 166: `border-top-left-radius:200px 100px`

Elliptical radius is set by specifying two values for each axis on the same corner, separated by space.

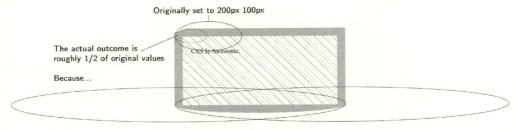

Figure 167: When using elliptical radius with extremely large values the curve of one corner can affect the curve of adjacent corners, especially ones with smaller radius values. This is where things get a bit unpredictable. But the good thing is that this level of looseness opens room for more creative experimentation. You just have to play around with different values to achieve a certain effect or a curve you're looking for.

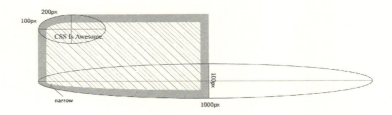

Figure 168: The principle behind applying large values to the elliptical corners.

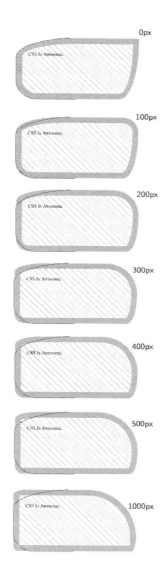

Figure 169: In this example, we are changing only the value of the upper right corner's curve. Notice however, that all rounded corners of the element are codependent to one another – even the ones whose values we are not changing explicitly.

17 2D Transforms

2D transforms can `translate`, `scale` or `rotate` an HTML element.

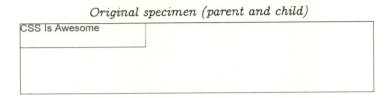

Figure 170: We'll use this simple HTML element specimen to demonstrate 2D CSS transforms.

17.1 translate

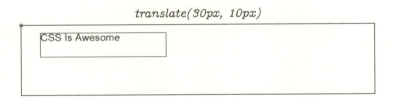

Figure 171: Instead of using top and left properties, we can use `transform:translate(30px,10px)` to move the element on its X and Y axis.

17.2 rotate

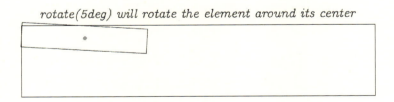

Figure 172: Rotating an element around its center using `rotate(angle)`, where *angle* is an angle between 0 and 360 degrees, with "deg" appended.

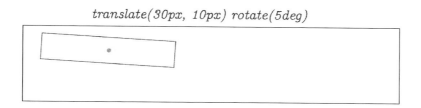

Figure 173: It's possible to translate and rotate an element.

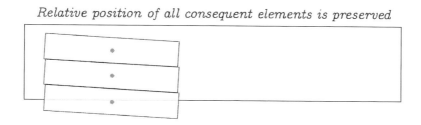

Figure 174: Three elements with `display:block;position:relative;` set to the same angle.

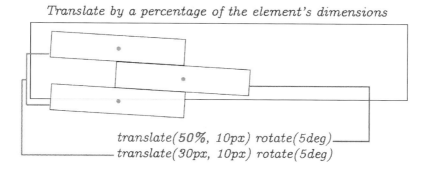

Figure 175: Translate transform can take a percentage of the element's size.

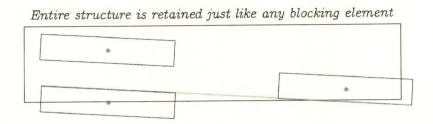

Figure 176: Relative elements retain their position within the document even after rotation.

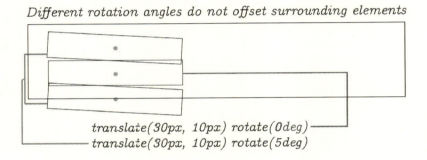

Figure 177: Rotating an element between others does not affect their position. The edges will overlap.

The order of translate and rotate does not matter

translate(30px, 10px) rotate(5deg) is the same as:
rotate(5deg) translate(30px, 10px)

Figure 178: The order is irrelevant.

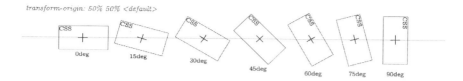

Figure 179: Rotate transform will rotate the element around its midpoint by default.

17.3 transform-origin

Figure 180: Moving element rotation origin using `transform-origin:0 0;`

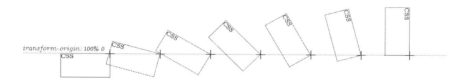

Figure 181: `transform-origin:100% 0`

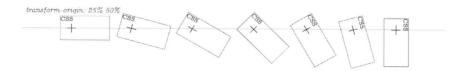

Figure 182: The rotation origin doesn't have to be in the middle or at the corners of the element. It can be anywhere.

18 3D Transforms

3D transforms can transform your regular HTML elements into 3D by adding perspective.

18.1 rotateX

Let's rotate the element on X-axis using `transform:rotateX`.

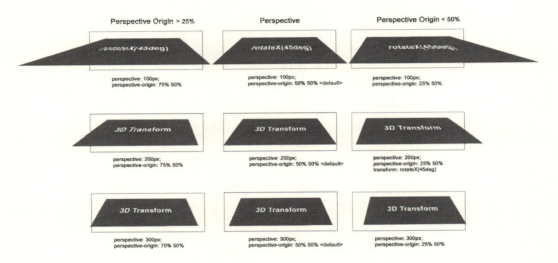

Figure 183: Each row in this example portrays what happens to an HTML element when its perspective is changed from 100px, to 200px and then to 300px from top down, using `perspective` property. The `perspective-origin` property is also used to demonstrate the slant created when the origin is displaced.

18.2 rotateY and rotateZ

Rotating the element on Y and Z axis produces these results:

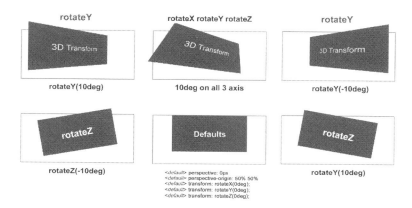

Figure 184: Rotating on the Y and Z axis.

18.3 scale

Scaling an element either reduces or increases its relative size on any of the 3 axis.

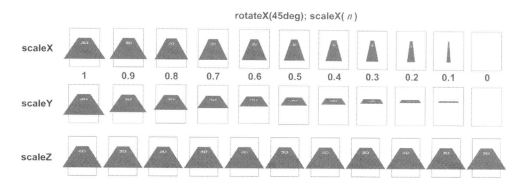

Figure 185: Likewise, you can "scale" an element on any of the 3 axis. Scaling on Z axis does not change the element's appearance when no perspective is set.

18.4 translate

You can translate an element in 3 dimensions. This diagram explains what happens when an element is translated on either X, Y or Z axis. Note that the camera is facing down the negative Z axis. So, scaling an element on Z axis up will make it appear "closer" to the view. In other words, its size will increase as it moves closer toward the camera.

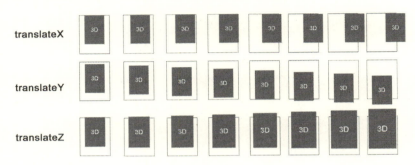

Figure 186: Translating an element across 3 axis – X, Y and Z.

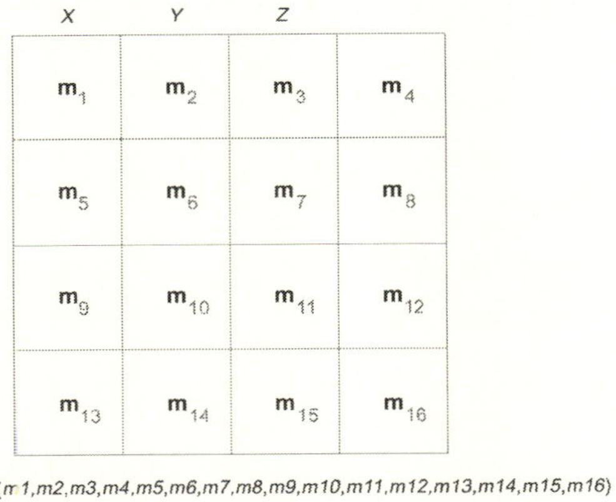

Figure 187: CSS provides a "matrix" consisting of a 4 x 4 grid. How 3D matrices work is outside the scope of this book. But basically, they modify the perspective. They are often used in 3D video games to set up the camera view to look at the main character or "lock in" on a moving object.

18.5 Creating A 3D Cube

Let's take our knowledge of 3D transforms in CSS and construct a 3-dimensional cube from 6 HTML elements.

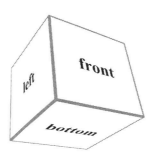

Figure 188: A 3D cube made up from 6 HTML elements, each translated by half of its width and rotated 90 degrees in all directions.

```
<div class="view">                              .view {
    <div class="cube">                              width: 200px;
        <div class="face front">front</div>         height: 200px;
        <div class="face back">back</div>           perspective: 300px;
        <div class="face right">right</div>      }
        <div class="face left">left</div>
        <div class="face top">top</div>
        <div class="face bottom">bottom</div>
    </div>
</div>
```

Figure 189: This is our setup. It's simply 6 HTML elements, each with a unique class and 3D transforms.

Let's build the cube!

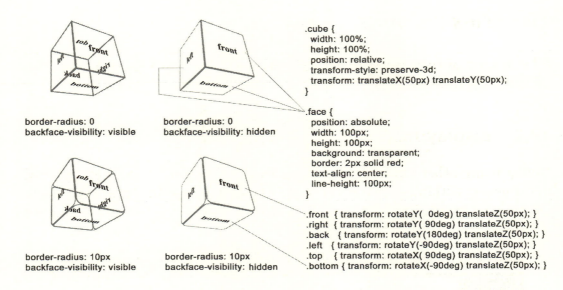

Figure 190: By rotating each face around the hypothetical center of the cube, we can construct this 3D object.

Note here `backface-visibility` property was set to hidden, to hide elements that are facing away from the camera. This makes our cube appear solid.

19 Flex

Flex is a set of rules for automatically stretching multiple columns and rows of content across parent container.

19.1 display:flex

Unlike many other CSS properties, in Flex you have a main container and items nested within it. Some CSS flex properties are used only on the parent. Others only on the items.

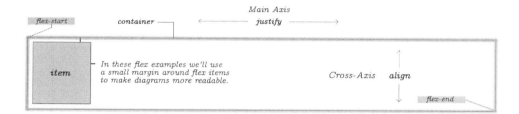

Figure 191: You can think of a flex element as a parent container with `display:flex`. Elements placed inside this container are called items. Each container has a `flex-start` and `flex-end` points as shown on this diagram.

19.2 Main-axis and Cross-axis

While the list of items is provided in a linear way, Flex requires you to be mindful of rows and columns. For this reason, it has two coordinate axis. The horizontal axis is referred to as *Main-Axis* and the vertical is the *Cross-Axis*.

To control the behavior of content's width and gaps between that stretch horizontally across the Main-Axis you will use *justify* properties. To control vertical behavior of items you will use *align* properties.

If you have 3 columns and 6 items, a second row will be automatically created by Flex to accommodate for the remaining items.

If you have more than 6 items listed, even more rows will be created.

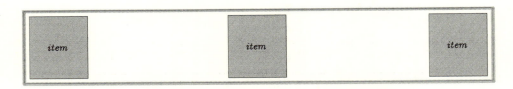

Figure 192: Flex items equally distributed on the Main-Axis. We'll take a look at the properties and values to accomplish this in just a moment.

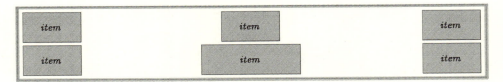

Figure 193: You can determine the number of columns.

How the rows and columns are distributed inside the parent element is determined by CSS Flex properties `flex-direction`, `flex-wrap` and a few others that will be demonstrated throughout the rest of this chapter.

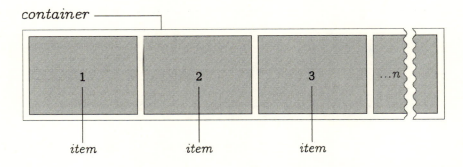

Figure 194: Here we have an arbitrary n-number of items positioned within a container. By default, items stretch from left to right. However, the origin point can be reversed.

19.3 Direction

It's possible to set direction of the item's flow by reversing it.

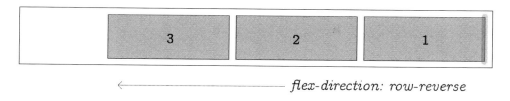

Figure 195: `flex-direction:row-reverse` changes direction of the item list flow. The default is `row`, which means flowing from left to right, as you would expect!

19.4 Wrap

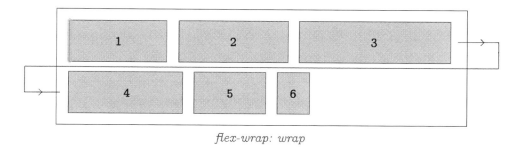

Figure 196: `flex-wrap:wrap` determines how items are wrapped when parent container runs out of space.

19.5 Flow

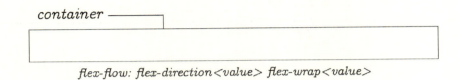

Figure 197: `flex-flow` is a short hand for `flex-direction` and `flex-wrap` allowing you to specify both of them using just one property name.

Figure 198: `flex-flow:row wrap` determines `flex-direction` to be `row` and `flex-wrap` to be `wrap`.

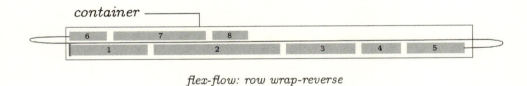

Figure 199: `flex-flow:row wrap-reverse;`

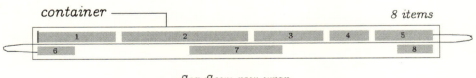

Figure 200: `flex-flow:row wrap; justify-content: space-between;`

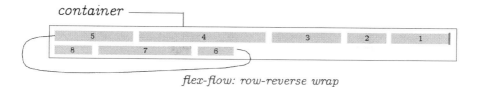

flex-flow: row-reverse wrap

Figure 201: `flex-flow:row-reverse wrap;`

flex-flow: row-reverse wrap-reverse

Figure 202: `flex-flow:row-reverse wrap-reverse;`

flex-flow: row wrap
justify-content: space-between

Figure 203: `flex-flow:row wrap; justify-content:  space-between;`

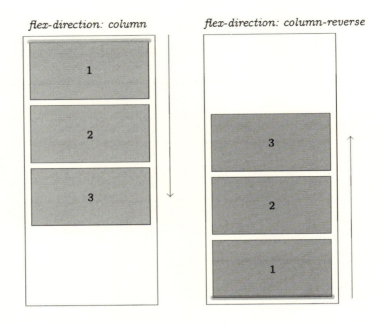

Figure 204: The direction can be changed to make the Cross-Axis primary. When we change flex direction to `column`, the flex-flow property behaves in exactly the same way as in previous examples. Except this time, they follow the vertical direction of a column.

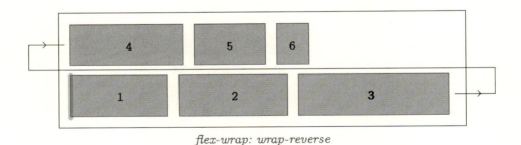

Figure 205: `flex-wrap:wrap-reverse`

19.6 justify-content: *value*

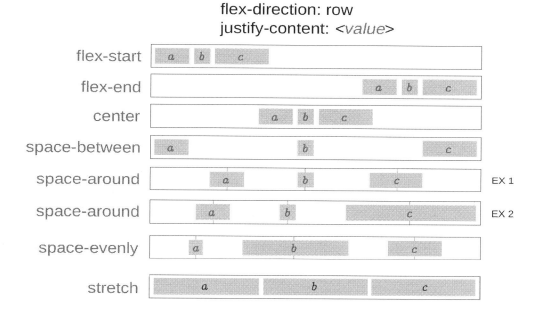

Figure 206: `flex-direction:row; justify-content:` *flex-start — flex-end — center — space-between — space-around — stretch — space-evenly*. In this example we're using only 3 items per row. There is no limit on the number of items you wish to use in flex. These diagrams only demonstrate the behavior of items when one of the listed values is applied to `justify-content` property.

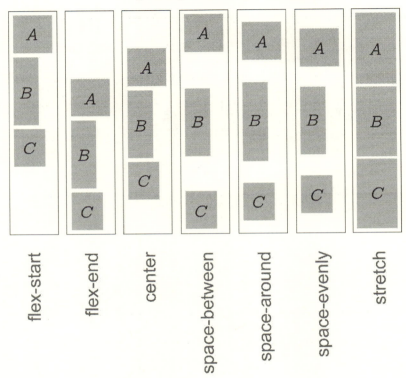

Figure 207: The same `justify-content` property is used to align items when `flex-direction` is column.

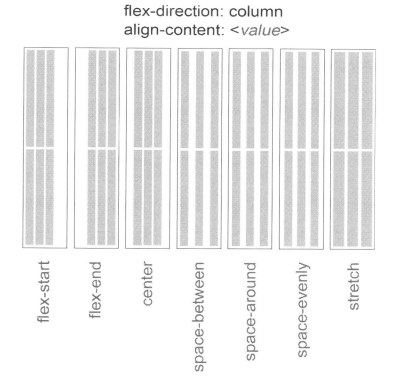

Figure 208: In CSS documentation this is referred to as packing flex lines. In this example `flex-direction` is set to `column`.

19.7 align-items

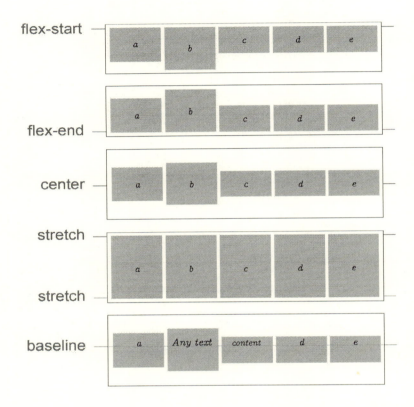

Figure 209: `align-items` controls the align of items horizontally, relative to the parent container.

19.8 flex-basis

Figure 210: `flex-basis` works similar to another CSS property: `min-width` outside of flex. It will expand item's size based on the size of inner content. Otherwise the default *basis* value will be used.

19.9 flex-grow

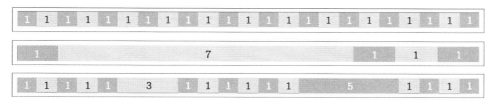

Figure 211: `flex-grow`, when applied to an item will scale it relative to the sum of the size of all other items on the same row, which are automatically adjusted according the the value that was specified. In each example here the item's flex-grow value was set to 1, 7 and (3 and 5) in the last example.

19.10 flex-shrink

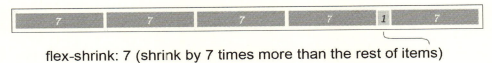

flex-shrink: 7 (shrink by 7 times more than the rest of items)

Figure 212: `flex-shrink` is the opposite of `flex-grow`. In this example value of 7 was used to "shrink" the selected item in the amount of time equal to 1/7th times the size of its surrounding items – which it will be also automatically adjusted.

.item { flex: none | [flex-grow | flex-shrink | flex-basis] }

Figure 213: When dealing with individual items, you can use the property `flex` as a shortcut for `flex-grow`, `flex-shrink` and `flex-basis` using only one property name.

19.11 order

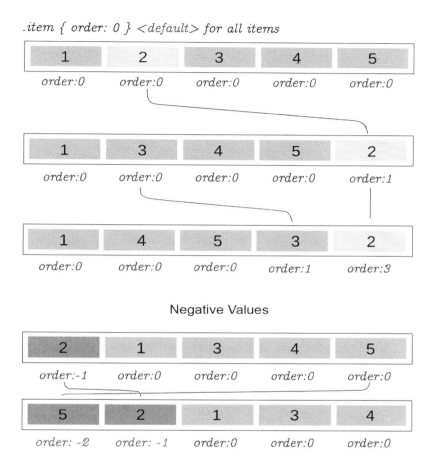

Figure 214: Using `order` property it's possible to re-arrange the natural order of items.

19.12 justify-items

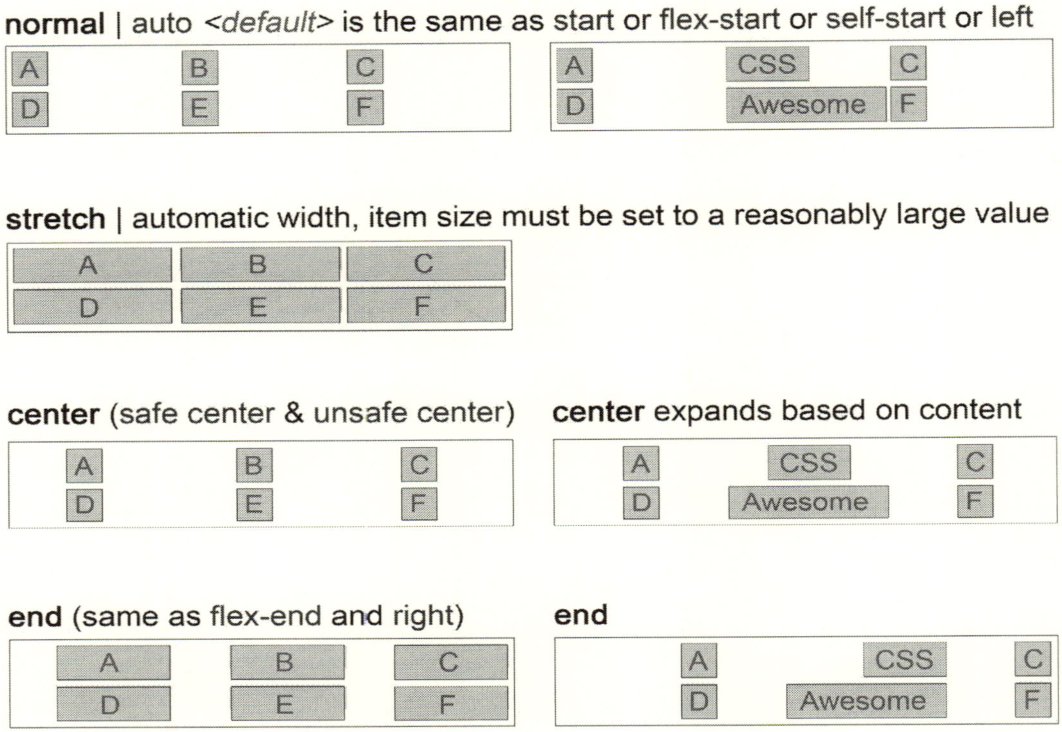
normal | auto <default> is the same as start or flex-start or self-start or left
A B C D E F
A CSS C D Awesome F
stretch | automatic width, item size must be set to a reasonably large value
A B C D E F
center (safe center & unsafe center)
A B C D E F
center expands based on content
A CSS C D Awesome F
end (same as flex-end and right)
A B C D E F
end
A CSS C D Awesome F

Figure 215: `justify-items` is similar to Flex's `justify-content` but for CSS grid, which is our next subject.

19.13 Interactive Flex Editor

As the name suggests, Flex provides layout elements that *dynamically* respond to the dimensions of parent container. But that also makes it difficult to explain the full scope of its capabilities in print.

I've been contacted by more than one teacher, saying that this tool is used to teach Flex in the classroom.

Head over to http://www.csstutorial.org/flex-both.html to play around with this interactive flex editor.

This editor is also used by developers who don't want to retype redundant HTML code just to create a new flex layout – you can use this editor to create your layout and copy the HTML code with a click of a button!

20 CSS Grid

20.1 CSS Grid Model

If there *were* a CSS Grid Box Model, it would probably look like this:

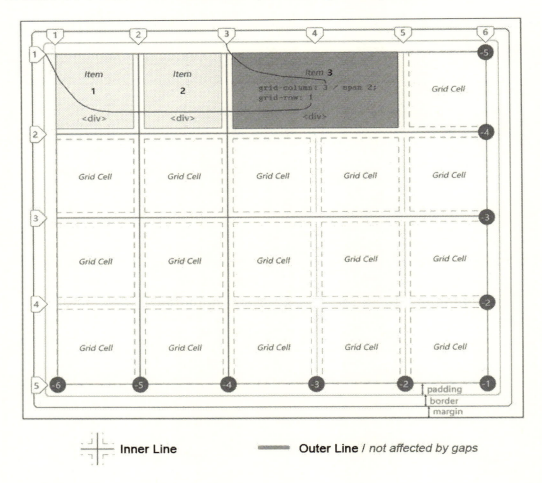

The grid itself is only a ***logistical scaffold*** of space broken down into cells. It's up to the designer to provide enough inner items / cells in order to determine a particular area of the website or web application.

The darker circles are indicative of the negative coordinate system, that starts at [-1, -1] in the lower right corner.

21 CSS Grid – Using Template Areas

Template areas have already been discussed in a previous section, but how can we utilize them in order to build an actual layout?

Keep in mind that CSS Grid was designed with an open mind for creativity. There isn't any one formula or pattern that should be followed.

A common technique you will naturally discover is splitting up your layout into areas using `grid-template-areas` and providing area names for each row in string format as shown in the following example:

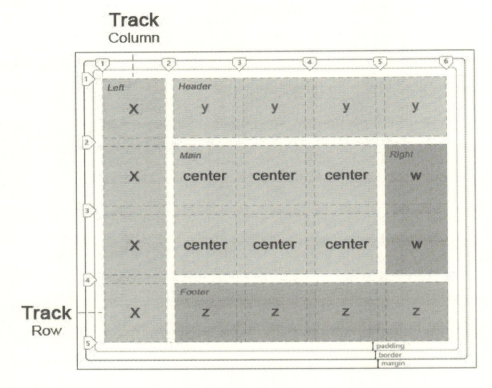

Figure 216: You cannot create irregular-shaped areas. They have to be square or rectangular.

This grid layout can be created as follows:

```
div#grid {
    display: grid;
    grid-template-areas:

        'x y y y y'
        'x center center center w'
        'x center center center w'
        'x z z z z';
}
```

And the accompanying HTML:

```
<div id = "grid">
    <div style = "grid-area: x"> Left </div>
    <div style = "grid-area: y"> Header </div>
    <div style = "grid-area: z"> Footer </div>
    <div style = "grid-area: w"> Right </div>
    <div style = "grid-area: center"> Main </div>
</div>
```

Template Areas work well for creating the primary outer scaffold for your layout. Often web developers assign `display:flex` to the inner cells.

21.1 CSS Grid & Media Queries

21.1.1 Media Queries

Media queries are similar to *if*-statements.

They start with the `@media` rule and specify a condition in parenthesis.

21.1.2 Changing content based on browser size

One of the most common use cases for media queries is doing something based on current browser dimensions. This means that they are often used as the first go-to choice for **creating responsive layouts**.

When used in this way **media queries** imitate the **onresize** event in JavaScript except you don't have to write any event callbacks yourself.

During my job interview at a Texas software company back in 2017 the team lead has introduced me to the idea that computer scientists (and probably scientists in general) make progress by "filling in the gaps."

That idea stuck with me.

I don't know but maybe like me, you found yourself trying to fill in the gaps learning CSS grid. Just as it ought to happen, every time some new tech emerges on the unsuspecting JavaScript crowd.

This tutorial was created by applying this ideology in preparation for working on the Visual Dictionary – the book you are reading right now – my post-mortem to CSS. This is when I decided to take all of the existing 413 CSS properties and visualize them by making diagrams.

While primarily I consider myself a JavaScript programmer I'd like to think that I also lean a bit toward the graphic design mindset as well. Perhaps I took the idea of gaps out of context when I applied it to CSS grid in this tutorial.

But bear with me.

As professional book designers may already know, the key to *CSS grid* lies in grasping not the visible parts of layout design but ones that are not.

Let me explain.

Book designers care about margins – essentially an invisible element of book design. It may not seem like much but remove margins – the element that the reader is least aware of – and the whole reading experience turns awkward.

Readers notice lack of margins only when they are absent. Therefore – as a designer (of anything) it is imperative to pay equal attention to the invisible elements of design.

We can always just plug in the content into the layout. Could it be then... that when we design with *CSS grid*, all we're doing here to create beautiful layouts is working with an advanced version of book margins? Could be.

The gaps.

Of course CSS grid goes way beyond designing margins in books but the principle of the so-called invisible design remains the same. Things we cannot see are important. In CSS grid this concept is thought of as gaps.

A CSS grid after all is just like taking book margins to the next level. Sort of.

21.2 Creating Your First CSS Grid

Much like Flex, CSS grid properties are never applied to just one element. The grid works as a single unit, consisting of a parent element and items contained within it.

First... we will need a container and some items.

A CSS grid flow can go in either direction. But by default it's set to row.

This means that if all other defaults are untouched your items will automatically form a single row where each item inherits its width from the grid's container element:

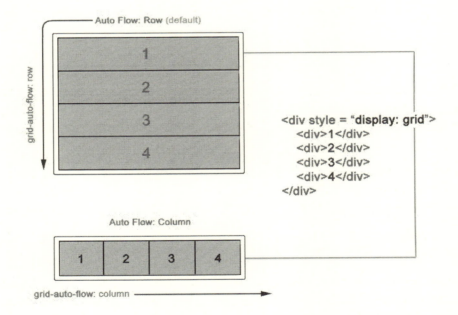

Figure 217: Just like Flex, CSS Grid can align items in one of the either `direction:rows` or columns specified by `grid-auto-flow` property.

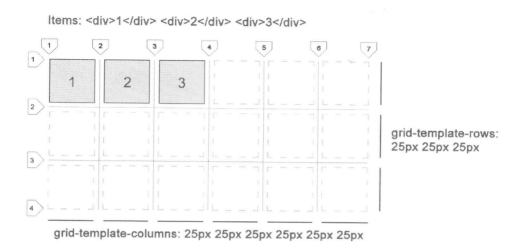

Figure 218: The CSS grid creates a virtual grid environment, where the items don't have to fill up the entire area of the grid. But the more items you add, the more placeholders will become available to populate the grid. CSS grid just makes this automatic process a bit more graceful.

The CSS grid uses column and row templates to choose how many items will be used in your grid down and across. You can specify their number by using CSS properties `grid-template-rows` and `grid-template-columns` respectively as shown on the diagram above. This is the basic construct of CSS grid.

One thing you will notice about CSS grid right away is the definition of gaps. This is different from what we've seen in any other CSS property before. Gaps are defined numerically starting from the upper left corner of the element.

There are **columns + 1** gaps between columns and similarly, **rows + 1** gaps between rows. As you would expect.

CSS grid does not have a default *padding*, *border*, or *margin* and all of its items are assumed to be `content-box` by default. Meaning, content is padded on the inside of the item, not outside like in all other common blocking elements.

That's one of the best things about CSS grid in general. Finally we have a new layout tool that treats its box model as `content-box` by default.

CSS grid's gap size can be set individually per row or column when you use properties `grid-row-gap` and `grid-column-gap`. Or, for convenience... together by just one property `grid-gap` as a shorthand.

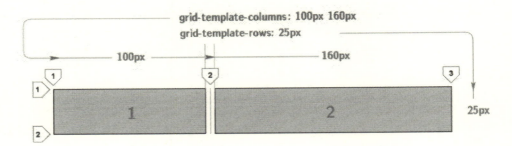

Figure 219: Here I created a miniature grid consisting of one row and 2 columns. Note the wedges here specify horizontal and vertical gaps between the items. In all future diagrams from now on, these wedges will be used to illustrate gaps. Gaps are a bit different than borders or margins, in that the outside of the grid area is not padded by them.

To start getting to know CSS grid, let's take a look at this first simple example (Figure 3 from above). Here we have `grid-template-columns` and `grid-template-rows` CSS properties defining basic CSS grid layout. These properties can take multiple values (which you should separate by space) that in turn become columns and rows. Here we used these properties to define a minimalist CSS grid composed of two columns (100px 160px) and one row (25px.) In addition, the gaps on the outside border of the grid container do not add extra padding even when gap size is defined. Therefore they should be thought of as defined right on the edge. The gaps in between columns and rows – on the other hand – are the only ones that are affected by gap size.

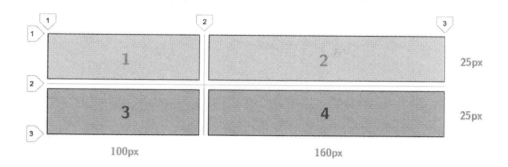

Figure 220: Adding more items into a CSS grid whose row template does not provide enough room to place them will *automatically* extend the CSS grid to open up more space. Here items 3 and 4 were added to previous example. But the `grid-template-columns` and `grid-template-rows` properties provide a template only for 2 items maximum.

21.3 Implicit Rows and Columns

CSS grid then adds them into *implicit* placeholders that it creates automatically, even if they were not specified as part of the grid template.

Implicit (I also like to call them *automatic*) placeholders inherit their width and height from the existing template.

They simply extend the grid area when necessary. Usually, when the number of items is unknown. For example, when a callback returns from talking to a database grabbing a number of images from a product profile.

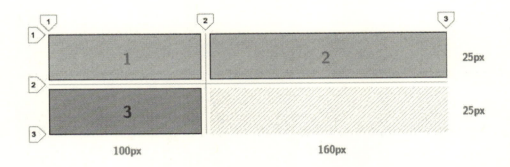

Figure 221: In this example we have an implicitly added placeholder for item 3. But because there is no item 4, the last placeholder is not occupied, leaving the grid unevenly balanced.

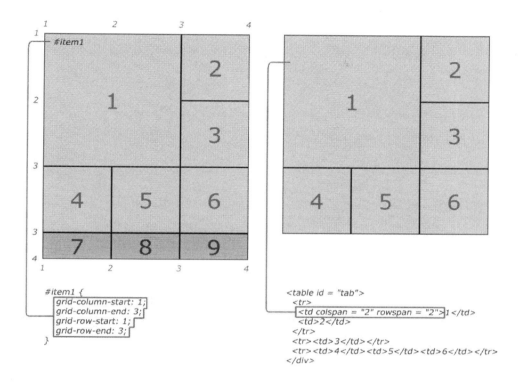

Figure 222: CSS grid should never be compared or used in the same way as a table. But it's interesting to note that a CSS grid inherits some design from the HTML table. In fact, the similarities are incredible upon a closer analysis. On the left hand side you are seeing a grid layout. Here `grid-column-start`, `grid-column-end`, `grid-row-start` and `grid-row-end` provide the same function of table's `colspan` and `rowspan`. The difference is that CSS grid uses the gap space in between to determine the span areas. Later you will also see that there is a shortcut for this. Note that here items 7, 8 and 9 were added implicitly, because the span occupied by the item 1 on the grid has pushed 3 items out of the original grid template layout. A table would never do this.

21.4 grid-auto-rows

The `grid-auto-rows` property tells CSS grid to use a specific height for *automatic* (implicitly created) rows. Yes, they can be set to a different value!

Instead of inheriting from `grid-template-rows` we can tell CSS grid to use a specific height for all implicit rows that fall outside of your default definitions.

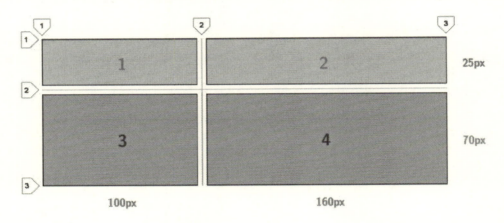

Figure 223: Implicit row height is determined by `grid-auto-rows`.

Bear in mind — of course — you can still set all of the values explicitly yourself, as shown in the following example:

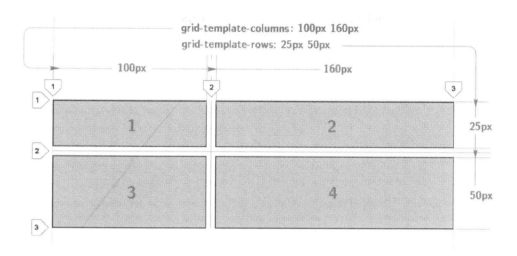

Figure 224: Explicitly specifying dimensions of all rows and columns.

In a way, CSS grid's `grid-auto-flow:column` invites *Flex-like* functionality:

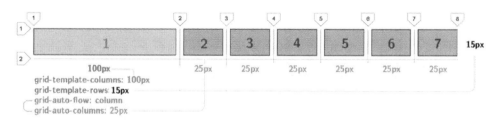

Figure 225: You can make your CSS grid behave similar to Flex by overwriting its `grid-auto-flow` property's default value of row to column. Note that here in this example we also used `grid-auto-columns: 25px` to determine the width of consecutive columns. This works in the same way as `grid-auto-rows` in one of the previous examples except this time the items are stretched horizontally.

21.5 Automatic Column Cell Width

CSS grid is excellent for creating traditional website layouts with two smaller columns on each side. There is an easy way to do this. Simply provide auto as a value to one of the widths in your `grid-template-column` property:

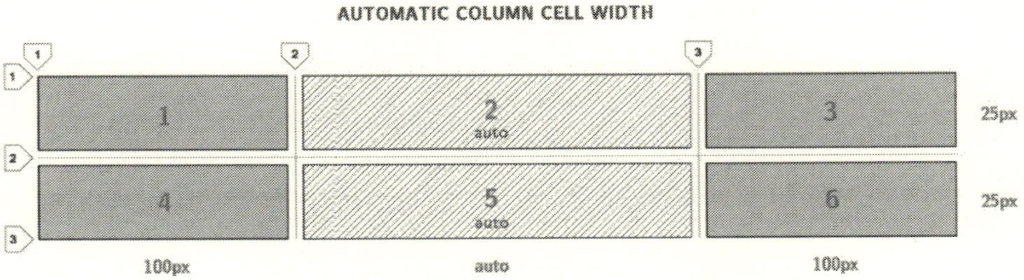

AUTOMATIC COLUMN CELL WIDTH

Figure 226: This is what happens with `grid-template-columns: 100px auto 100px`

Your grid will span across the entire width of the container or the browser.

As you can see already CSS grid offers a wide variety of properties to help you get creative with your website or application layout! I really like where this is going so far.

21.6 Gaps

Look, it's those gaps again.

We already talked about the gaps. Mostly just the fact that they *cover the space between columns and rows*. But we haven't talked about actually changing them.

The set of diagrams that follows will provide visual clues as to how gaps modify the appearance of your CSS grid.

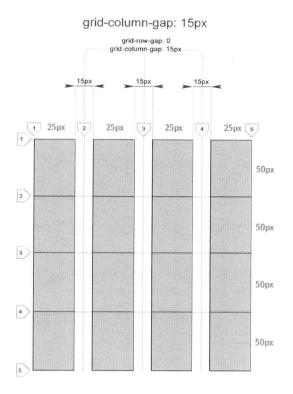

Figure 227: CSS grid has a property `grid-column-gap`, which is used to specify vertical gaps of equal size between all columns in your CSS grid.

I intentionally left the horizontal gaps clasped to their default value of 0, because they're not being discussed in this example.

I can already envision a Pinterest-like design with multiple columns using the setup above.

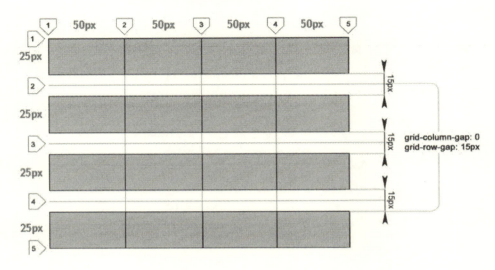

Figure 228: Likewise, using `grid-row-gap` property we can set horizontal gaps for the entire grid.

This is the same thing, except with horizontal gaps.

Using `grid-gap` property we can set gaps in both dimensions at the same time:

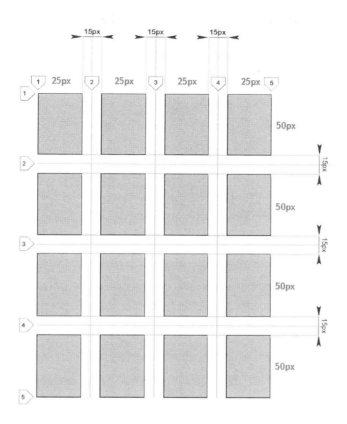

Figure 229: It is possible to set the gaps on entire CSS grid by using shorthand property `grid-gap`. But this means that gaps in both dimensions will be set to the same value. In this example it is `15px`.

And finally... you can set gaps individually for each of the two dimensions.

The next 3 diagrams were created to demonstrate the different possibilities made of using the CSS grid that can be useful in various cases.

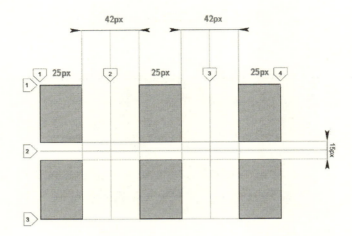

Figure 230: Here gaps are set individually per row and column which allows for varied column design. In this example wide column gaps are used. You can probably use this strategy for crafting *image galleries* for wide-screen layouts.

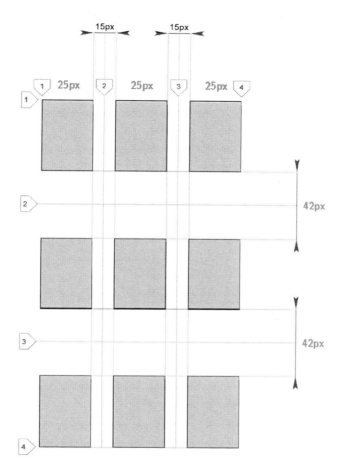

Figure 231: Here is the same thing as the previous example. Except we're using wider row gaps.

One thing I was disappointed about was the lack of support for the ability to create varied gap sizing within the same dimension. I think this is the most daunting limitation of CSS grid. And I hope in the future it gets fixed.

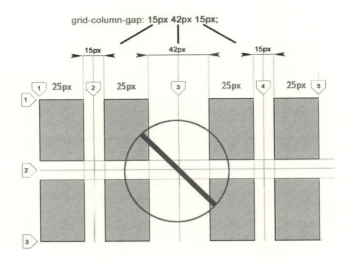

Figure 232: This layout cannot be created using CSS grid. Varied gap sizing is currently (June 2nd, 2018) not a possibility with CSS grid.

21.7 fr – Fractional Unit – for efficiently sizing the remaining space.

One *somewhat* recent addition to CSS language is the *fr* unit.

The *fr* units can be used on things other than CSS grid. But in combination with one they are magical for creating layouts with unknown screen resolution... and still preserve proportion without thinking in percent.

The *fr* unit is similar to percentage values in CSS (25%, 50%, 100%... etc) except represented by a fractional value (0.25, 0.5, 1.0...)

But although it could be *1fr* is not always 100%. The *fr* unit automatically dissects remaining space. The easiest way to demonstrate this is by following diagrams.

Here is a basic example of using *fr* units:

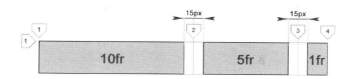

Figure 233: An example of using the *fr* CSS unit.

This is great news for intuitive designers.

1fr will be 10/1 of *10fr* regardless of how much space *10fr* takes up. It's all relative.

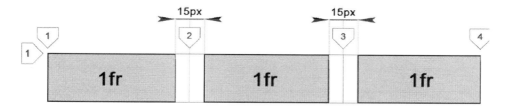

Figure 234: Using *1fr* to define 3 columns produces columns of equal width.

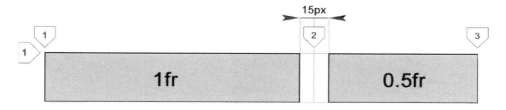

Figure 235: You can also use fractions.

Relative to *1fr*, *0.5fr* is exactly half of *1fr*.

These values are calculated relative to the parent container.

Can you mix percentage values with *1fr*? Of course you can!

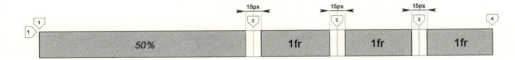

Figure 236: The example here demonstrates mixing % units with *fr*. The results are always intuitive and produce the effect you would expect.

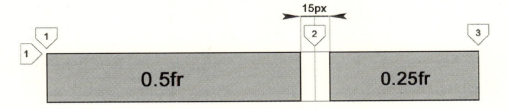

Figure 237: Fractional *fr* units are relative to themselves within some parent container.

21.8 Working With Fractional Units

Fractional Units (or *fr*-units) divide your layout segment into equal and relative parts. As we will see below, *1fr* isn't a specific unit like *px* or *em*, but *relative* to the remaining empty space.

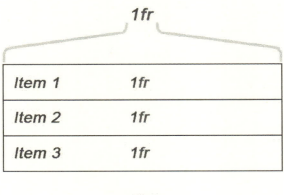

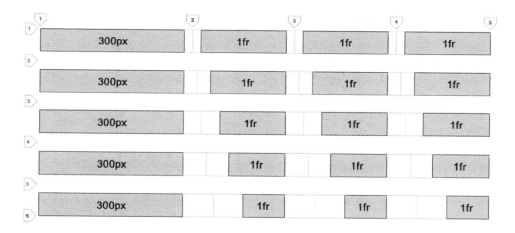

Figure 238: Using *1fr* units and increasing column gaps at the same time will produce this result. I just wanted to include this here to demonstrate that *1fr* units will be affected by gaps too. 5 different CSS grids used here to demonstrate how we should be also mindful of the gaps when designing with *1fr* units.

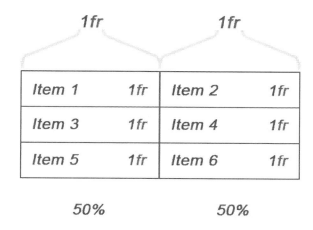

grid-template-columns:

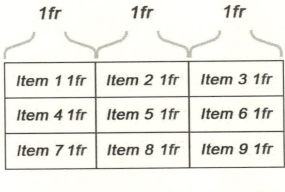

grid-template-columns: 1fr 10fr

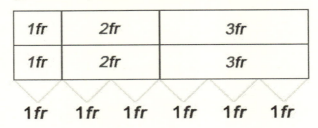

10fr = 1fr * 10

grid-template-columns: 1fr 2fr 3fr

1fr	2fr	3fr
1fr	2fr	3fr

1fr 1fr 1fr 1fr 1fr 1fr

22 Fractional Units & Gaps

Gaps affect *Fractional Units* because now, every time new **fr**-based column is added, we need to also subtract gaps from remaining space in the element.

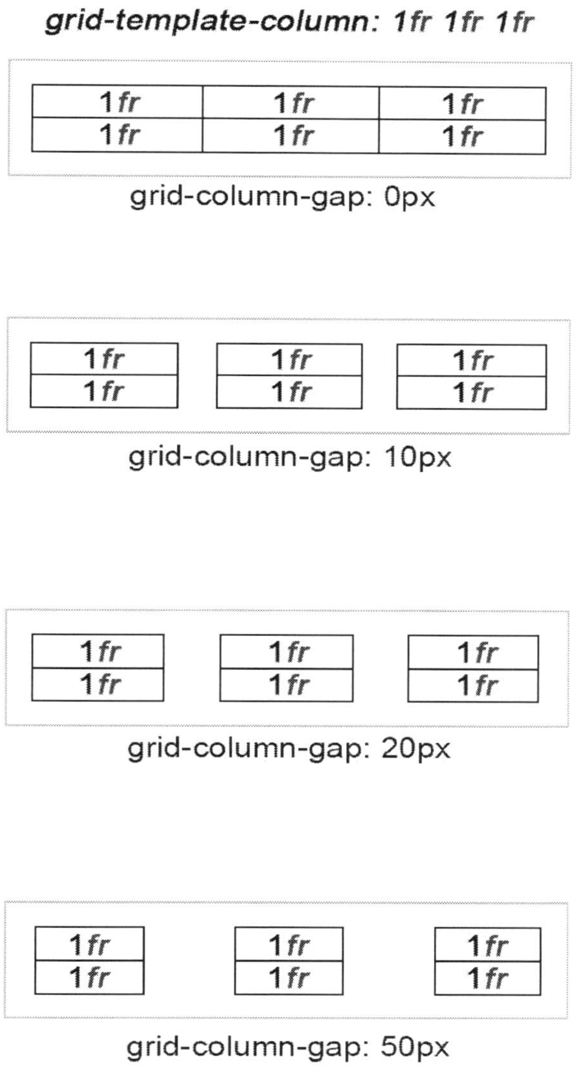

grid-template-column: 1fr 1fr 1fr

1fr	1fr	1fr
1fr	1fr	1fr

grid-column-gap: 0px

1fr		1fr		1fr
1fr		1fr		1fr

grid-column-gap: 10px

1fr		1fr		1fr
1fr		1fr		1fr

grid-column-gap: 20px

1fr		1fr		1fr
1fr		1fr		1fr

grid-column-gap: 50px

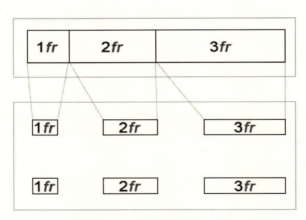

grid-column-gap: 100px

grid-template-column: 1fr 1fr 1fr

grid-column-gap: 50px;
grid-row-gap: 50px;

grid-column-gap: 50px;
grid-row-gap: 50px;

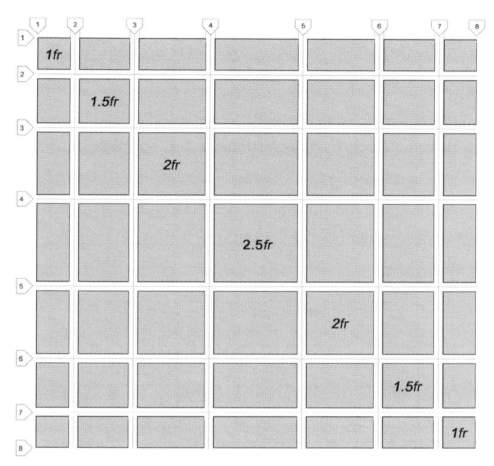

Figure 239: And just to be complete in our understanding of *fr* units, you can use them to create something like this. Although I don't know where you would require such a dinosauric layout it clearly demonstrates how *fr* units can affect both rows and columns.

22.1 Repeating Values

CSS grid allows the use of repeat property value.

The repeat property takes two values: times to repeat and what to repeat.

repeat(times, ... what);

At its basic this is how it works:

Figure 240: Here we're using `grid-template-columns` with repeat and without repeat to produce exactly the same effect. It is usually wise to choose the shortest path.

Here `grid-template-columns` are provided two different values to produce the same effect. Obviously repeat saves a lot of hassle here.

Final verdict: to save yourself from redundancy in cases where your grid must contain repetitive dimension values use repeat as a remedy. The `repeat` property can be sandwiched between other values, too.

Figure 241: `grid-template-columns:  50px repeat(3, 15px 30px) 50px`

In this example we repeat a section of two columns 15px 30px for 3 times in a row. I mean in a column. Ahh! You know what I mean.

22.2 Spans

Using CSS grid spans you allow your items to stretch across multiple rows or columns. This is a lot like `rowspan` and `colspan` in a `<table>`.

We will create a grid using repeat to avoid redundant values. But it could have been created without it — anyway, let's make it our specimen for this section.

When we add `grid-column:span` 3 to item #4 a somewhat unexpected effect has occurred: 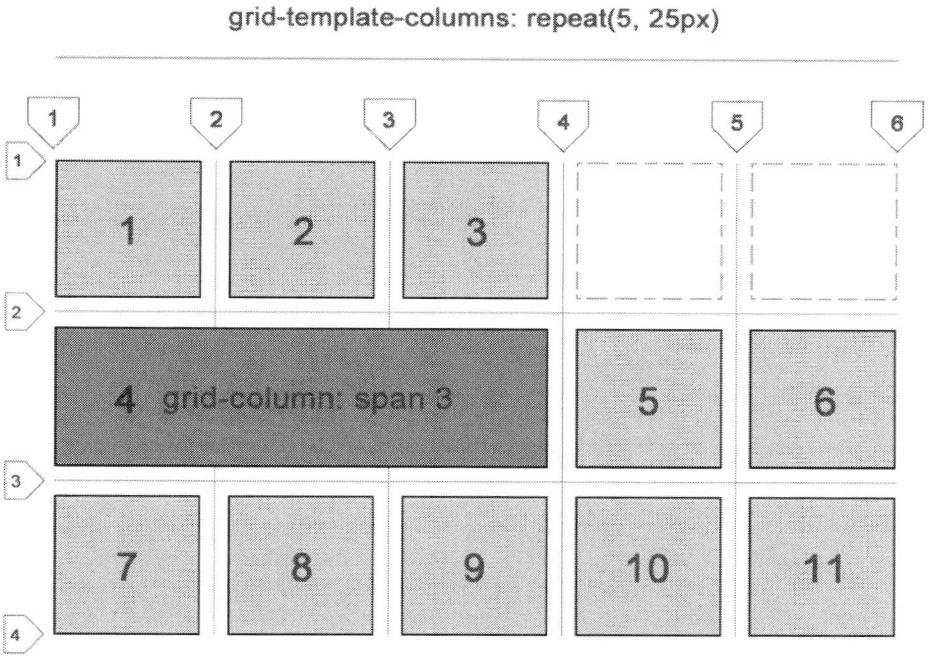

Figure 242: Using `grid-column:span` 3 to take up 3 columns. However, CSS grid makes a decision to remove some of the items, because the "spanned" item cannot fit into suggested area. Notice the blank squares!

In CSS grids spans can also be used to cover multiple rows. And if it so happened that the column is now greater in height than the height of the grid itself the CSS grid adapt itself to this:

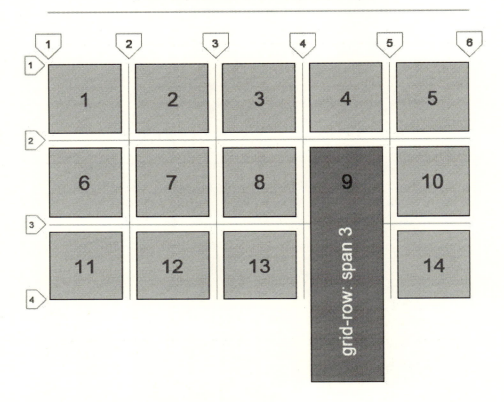

Figure 243: CSS grid is adapting itself in several cases where items go beyond grid's parent container.

You can also span across multiple rows and columns at the same time. I created this other minimalistic example just to quickly demonstrate limitations, even though in most cases this will probably not happen:

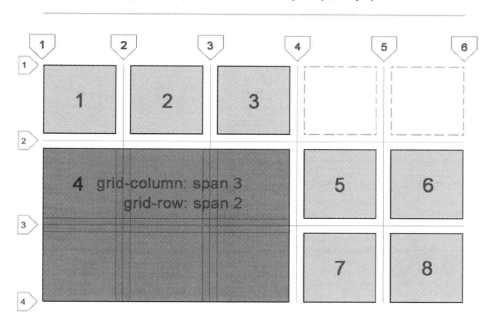

Figure 244: CSS grid fills in the blanks.

Pay attention to how CSS grid adapts to the items around spans that cover multiple rows and columns. All of the items still remain in the grid but intuitively wrap around other spanned items.

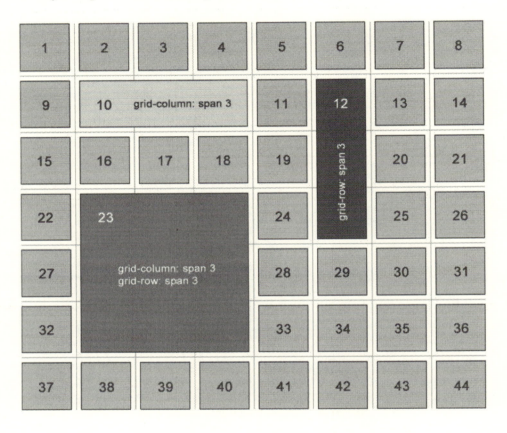

When I tried to break the layout with a large span I ended up with the following case that demonstrates the key limitations of CSS grid:

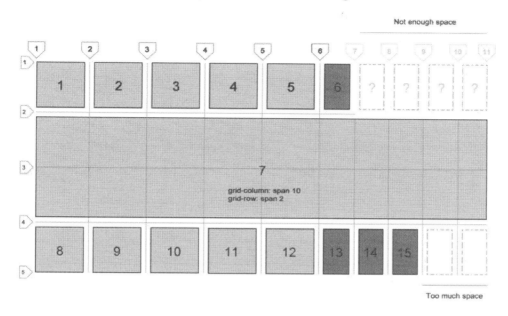

Figure 245: CSS grid replaces potential item cells with empty space in two distinct situations.

But it's still a lot like a ¡table¿. See my other CSS grid vs table tutorial where I show you the frightening similarities.

However... there is a solution.

22.3 Start and End

So far we used CSS grid *spans* to create multi-column and multi-row items that occupy a ton of space. But... CSS grid has another much more elegant solution to solve the same problem.

The `grid-row-start` and `grid-row-end` properties can be used to define the starting and ending point of an item on the grid Likewise, their column equivalents are `grid-column-start` and `grid-column-end`. The are also two shorthand properties: `grid-row:1/2` and `grid-column:1/2`.

174

These work an a slightly different way than *spans*.

With -start and -end properties, you can physically move your item to another location in the grid. Let's take a look at this minimalist example:

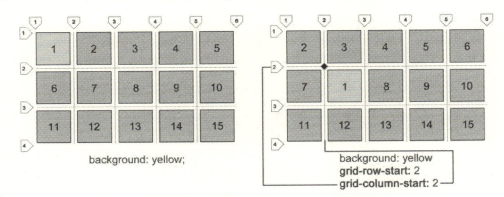

Figure 246: Using CSS grid's `grid-row-start` and `grid-column-start` on an item (first item in this example) you have the ability to physically move an item within your grid to another location!

Interestingly, designers of CSS grid have decided for the direction of the span vector to be insignificant. The span is still created within the specified area regardless of whether starting or ending points are provided in reverse order:

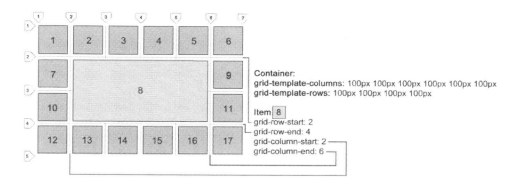

Figure 247: Here we've taken item 8 and (redundantly) specified its location using `grid-row-start` and `grid-column-start`. Notice however, this alone has no effect on item 8, because item 8 is already positioned at that location on the grid anyway. However, by doing this you can achieve span-like functionality if you also specify an ending location using `grid-column-end` and `grid-column-end`.

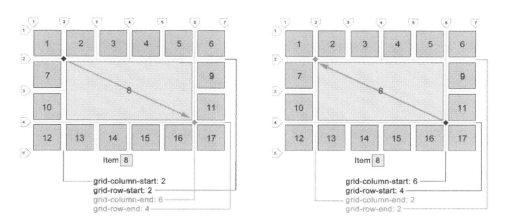

Figure 248: Specifying item span regardless of the direction of the start/end points produces the same results.

Let's consider this 6 x 4 CSS grid. If you explicitly specify an items's column end position that goes outside the number of specified columns (>=7) you will experience this wonky effect:

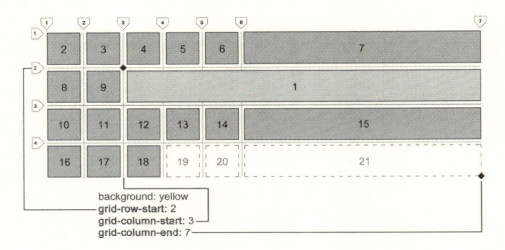

Figure 249: Making column width of an item greater than the original number of columns specified in the CSS grid.

In this case CSS grid will adapt the resulting layout of your grid to what you see in the example above. It's usually a good idea to design your layouts by being mindful of grid's boundaries to avoid these types of scenarios.

22.4 Start and End's Shorthand

You can use the shorthand properties `grid-row` and `grid-column` to same effect as above using / to separate values. Except instead of providing an end value, it takes width or height of the span:

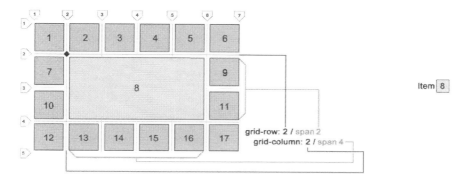

Figure 250: We can use / character for this short-hand syntax.

What if we need to reach the absolute maximum boundary of the grid?

Use `-1` to extend a column (or row) all the way to the end of CSS grid's size when number of columns or rows is unknown. But be mindful of any implicit items (16, 17) slipping away from the bottom of the grid:

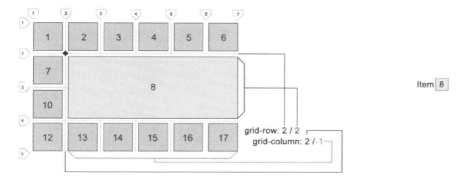

Figure 251: Using negative `-1` value to count from right-most gap to left.

Then I tried to do the same with rows, but the results were more chaotic, depending on which combinations of values I provided. I know there are other ways of using / but for the sake of clarity I want to keep things simple.

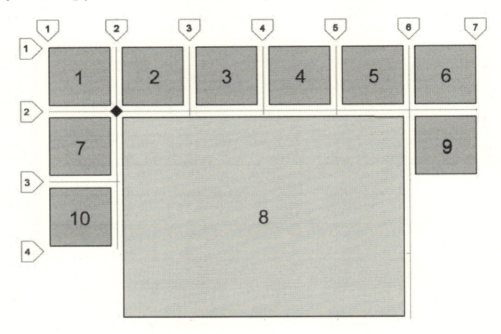

Figure 252: I only used 10 items in this example. CSS grid seems to gracefully resize itself.

When I was experimenting with rows to do the same thing, it seems like 4 in `grid-column:2/4` had to be changed to 2/6... but only if `grid-row:2/-1` was specified.

That puzzled me a bit. But I guess I still have a lot of learning to do on how /-separated values work.

What I found out though is that juggling around values here produced results that cannot be easily documented using visual diagrams.

Well, at least we get the basic idea here. You can extend either column or row all the way to the maximum boundary using -1. How one affects the other takes a bit of practice to figure out in some specific cases.

We can expand on this a bit. CSS grid has a secondary coordinate system, so to speak. And because it doesn't matter which direction you use to make cross-column and cross-row spans you can use negative values:

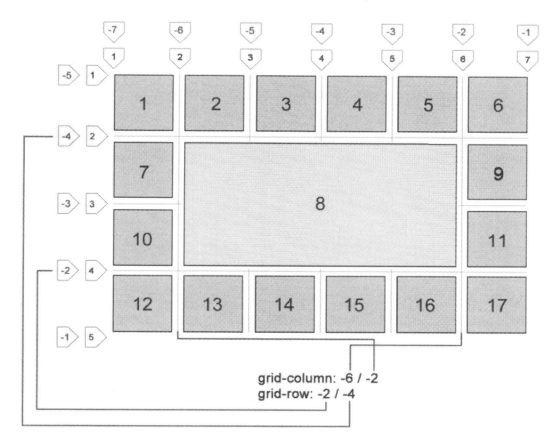

Figure 253: Using negative values to specify column and row's start and end, we can create the same span from previous examples, since CSS grid is coordinate system agnostic. You can use both positive and negative numbers!

As you can see CSS grid coordinate system is pretty flexible.

22.5 Content Align Within CSS Grid Items

Let's say you've gone to the great lengths mastering CSS grid item spans. You crossed the seas of implicitly generated rows and columns. Now you're curious to see what else is in store for you.

Good news for you then.

As a web designer, I've for a long time craved multi-directional float. I wanted to be able to float in the middle and on any corner of the container.

This functionality is only limited to CSS grids' `align-self` and `justify-self` and does not appear to work on any other HTML element. If your entire site's layout is built using a CSS grid then it solves a lot of issues associated with corner and center element placement.

22.6 align-self

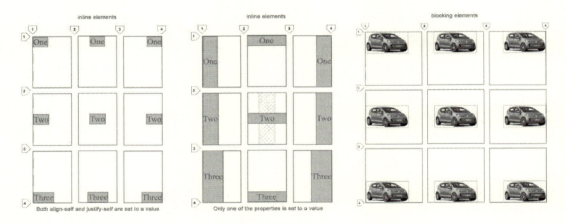

Figure 254: An example of using `align-self` and `justify-self` properties. The difference between the 9 squares is the combination of start and end values provided to the said properties to produce any of the results depicted above. I won't mention all of these combinations here, because it's quite intuitive.

VERTICAL: Use align-self: end to align the content to the bottom of the item. Likewise, align-self: start will make sure content sticks to the upper border.

HORIZONTAL: Use justify-self: start (or end) to justify your content left or right. In combination with align-self you can achieve placement depicted on any of the above examples.

Just to finalize this discussion here is how align-self affects a slightly more complex situation — one we've taken a look at before in this tutorial:

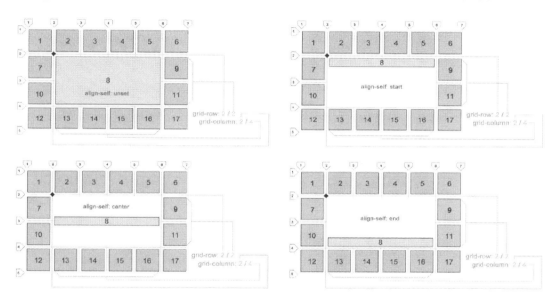

Figure 255: Using `align-self` it is possible to align the item's content with `start`, `center` and `end` values.

You can use values `start`, `center` and `end`.

Note, however there aren't `top` and `bottom` values for `align-self`.

22.7 justify-self

Another property that does the same thing but horizontally is `justify-self`:

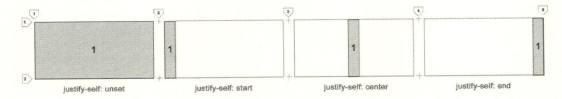

Figure 256: CSS grid item property justify-self in action using unset, start, center and end values.

You can use `start|left` or `end|right` values interchangeably here.

22.8 Template Areas

Template areas provide a way to refer to an isolated part of your grid by a predefined name. This name cannot include spaces. Use - instead.

Each set of row names is enclosed in double quotes. You can further separate these sets of row names either by a line break or by space to create columns as shown in the example below.

Although only 5 items are present template are names can logistically occupy places not yet filled with items:

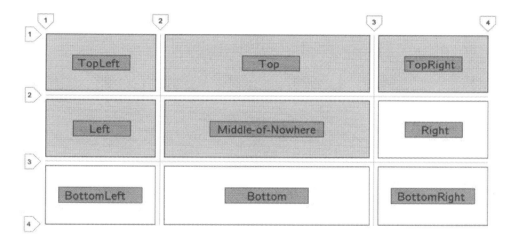

Figure 257: Example of specifying template areas with `grid-template-areas` property.

You can specify an area for any of the row and column as long as you separate the set of each consequent row by a space, and provide names for each row using double quotes. Within double quotes, each item is separated by space. This means *no spaces are allowed in template area names*.

Similar principle to specifying row and column size is followed here to name all of the areas in the grid. Just separate them by space or tab.

This syntax simply allows us to intuitively name our template areas.

But things get a lot more convenient when you start combining areas with the same name across multiple containers. Here I named 3 items in the left column Left and 3 items in the right column Right. CSS grid template areas automatically combined them to occupy the same space by name.

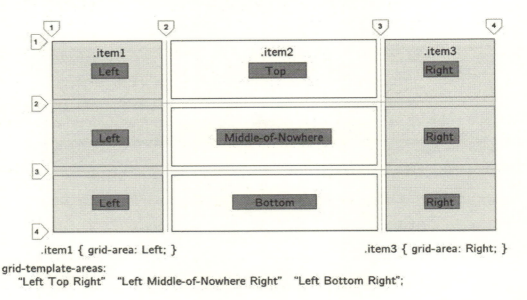

Figure 258: Spanning template areas across multiple grid "cells." Simply name your columns and rows, and adjacent blocks will "merge" into larger areas. Just make sure to keep them rectangular!

It's important to make sure that areas consist of items aligned into larger *rectangle* areas. **Doing Tetris blocks here will not work**. Straying from the rule of always keeping your areas rectangular is likely to break the CSS grid and/or produce unpredictable outcome.

22.9 Naming Grid Lines

Working with numbers (and negative numbers) can become redundant over time especially when dealing with complex grids. You can name grid lines with whatever you want using [name] brackets right before size value.

To name the first grid line you can: `grid-template-column:[left] 100px` Likewise for rows it is: `grid-template-row:[top] 100px`.

You can name multiple grid lines. The [] brackets are inserted at an intuitive place in the set. Exactly where the grid line (a.k.a. gap) would appear:

`grid-template-columns:[left] 5px 5px [middle] 5px 5px [right]`

Now you can use the names left, middle and right to refer to your grid lines when creating columns and rows that need to reach that area:

Naming gap lines creates a more meaningful experience. It's a lot better to think of the middle line as *center* (or *middle*) instead of 4. This tutorial covered almost everything there is to CSS grid using visual diagrams.

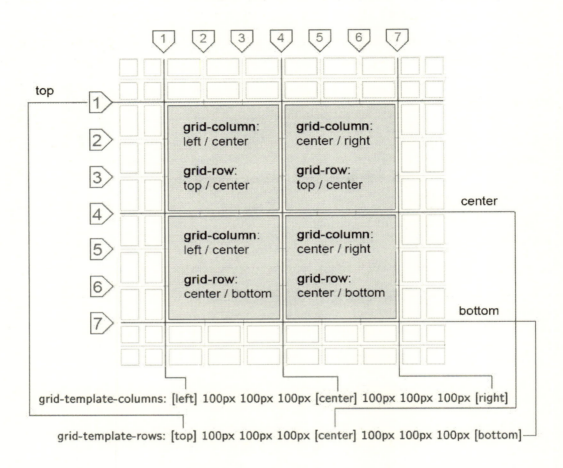

Figure 259: Instead of using numbers it is possible to name and refer to lines in between grid's cells as values to your properties `grid-template-columns` and `grid-template-rows`. Note how each span in the diagram refers to named lines and not the gap's numbers. You can use any name you want.

In conclusion... *remember...*

The music is not in the notes, but in the silence between – Wolfgang Amadeus Mozart

This seems to be true of CSS grid also. And so many other things!

Nearly 8 weeks have been spent drawing diagrams representing pretty much every single thing you can possibly do with CSS grid. And you've just looked at (and hopefully learned from) them all.

Of course, I assume the possibility that a few things were missed here and there. It's impossible to document absolutely every possible case. And I will be glad for anyone in the community to point it out so this book can be improved in the future editions with even more useful examples.

23 Animation

You can animate any CSS property whose physical **position**, **dimensions**, **angle** or **color** can be changed. Basic animation is surprisingly simple to implement using keyframes.

CSS animation keyframes are specified using the `@keyframes` directive. A *keyframe* is simply the element's state at a single point on animation time line.

CSS animation engine will automatically interpolate between animation keyframes. All you need to do is specify the state of CSS properties at the *start* and *end* points of the animation.

Once all of our *keyframe* locations are set up (*which are often specified in percent*) all we need to do is set up the defaults for our original element we wish to animate.

Then create a named animation using `@keyframes` *animationName* {...} format, that stores all the keyframes. We'll take a look at that in just a moment!

Finally, create a special class that will define your animation's **duration**, **direction**, **repeatability**, and **easing** type... and link it to the same animation name that was used by `@keyframes` directive.

This process is explained visually on the next page.

Let's turn a **yellow square** box into a **teal circle**.

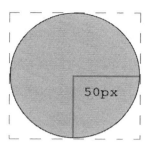

Orignal

width: 100px;
height: 100px;
border: 1px solid black;
background: yellow;

Target

border-radius: 50px;
background: teal;

```
@keyframes animationName {
    0% { border-radius: 0; background: yellow; }
  100% { border-radius: 50px; background: teal; }
}

.animateClass {
    animation-name: animationName;
    animation-fill-mode: forwards;
    animation: normal 3000ms ease;
}
```

Figure 260: Soon as .animateClass is assigned to an element, animation will start playing. The class has a link to animationName. It must match the name specified by @keyframes rule. This animation is set to last 3 seconds or 3000ms as specified. **Note:** Easing adds some flavor to your animation – by providing a curve describing relative velocity of your animation at a particular spot on the time line.

We'll cover *easing* and all other CSS animation properties throughout the remainder of this chapter, based on this simple example.

23.1 animation

The `animation` property is the *short-hand* to the 8 stand-alone animation properties described below:

`animation-name` – name of the keyframe specified by `@keyframes` directive.

`animation-duration` – duration of the animation in milliseconds.

`animation-timing-function` – specify easing function.

`animation-delay` – add delay before animation starts playing.

`animation-iteration-count` – number of times animation should play.

`animation-direction` – play forwards, backwards or alternate sequence.

`animation-fill-mode` – state of the animation when it is not playing.

`animation-play-state` – specify whether animation is `running` or is `paused`.

In the following sections we'll explore each one visually.

23.2 animation-name

The alpha-numeric animation identifier name:

```
001 .animationClass {
002     animation-name: animationName;
003     animation-fill-mode: normal;
004     animation: normal 3000ms ease-in;
005 }
```

Animation name must refer to the one specified by **@keyframes** directive:

```
001 @keyframes animationName {
002     0% { }
003     100% { }
004 }
```

23.3 animation-duration

You usually want to plan the length of your animation first.

Figure 261: You can specify duration in seconds or milliseconds, if you need more precision. For example **3000ms** is the same as **3s** and **1500ms** is the same as **1.5s**

23.4 animation-delay

If you don't want to start your animation right away you can add a delay.

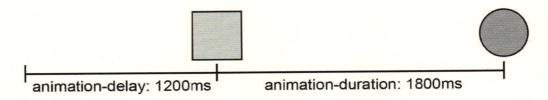

Figure 262: It is possible to assign a delay in milliseconds, before animation starts playing.

23.5 animation-direction

You can assign any of the four values to `animation-direction` property:

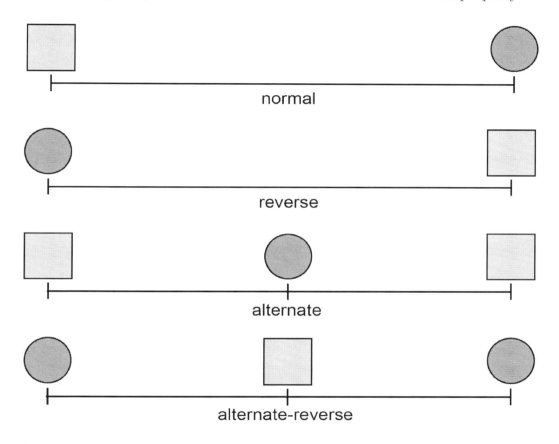

Figure 263: The values **normal**, **reverse**, **alternate** and **alternate-reverse**; and their effects.

CSS animation engine will automatically *interpolate* between frames. An interpolated animation state is simply any state between any two frames. As the color transitions from yellow to teal, it will gradually change over the period of time specified by the `animation` property (here, as a *short-hand*).

23.6 animation-iteration-count

Number of times animation will be repeated.

Figure 264: Play animation 1 time (default).

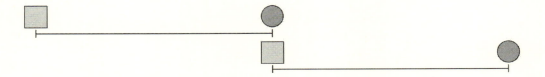

Figure 265: Repeat animation 2 times.

Figure 266: Repeat animation 3 times.

As you can see, the obvious problem here is that the animation will "jump" back to the first frame again.

You can use some of the other animation properties to make sure that this jumping doesn't occur. You can design your animation to loop, or tweak other properties based on particular UI dynamics you're looking for. This way you can design only "half" of your animation, and tweak properties to play it forwards or backwards, let's say on **mouse-in** and **mouse-out** events.

23.7 animation-timing-function

Easing is specified by `animation-timing-function`. It adds personality to your animation. This is done by adjusting velocity of the animation at any given point on the time line. Start, Middle and End points are of particular interest. Each easing type is defined by a **Bézier curve** function.

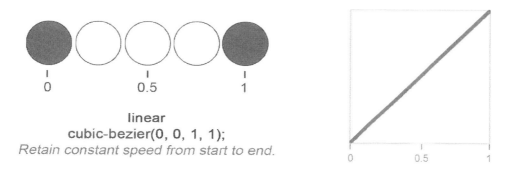

Figure 267: `animation-timing-function: linear;`

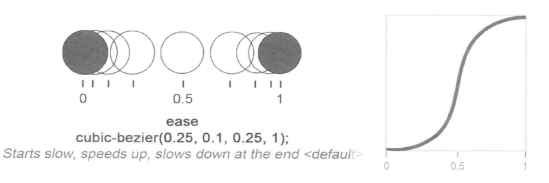

Figure 268: `animation-timing-function: ease;`

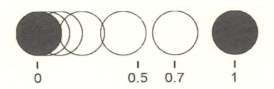 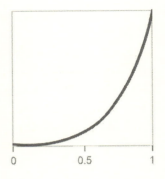

ease-in
cubic-bezier(0.42, 0, 1, 1);
Specifies a transition effect with a slow start.

Figure 269: `animation-timing-function: ease-in;`

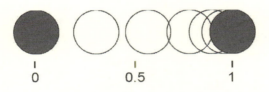 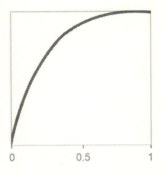

ease-out
cubic-bezier(0, 0, 0.58, 1);
Fast at first and gradually slow down toward the end.

Figure 270: `animation-timing-function: ease-out;`

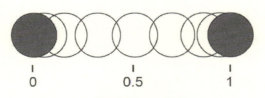 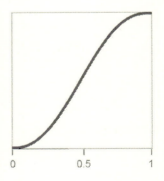

ease-in-out
cubic-bezier(0.42, 0, 0.58, 1);
Specifies a transition effect with a slow start and end.

Figure 271: `animation-timing-function: ease-in-out;`

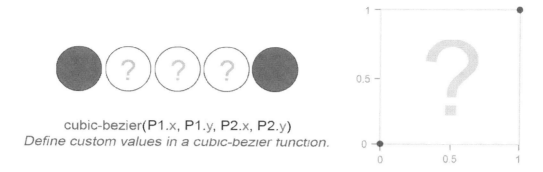

Figure 272: You can create your own cubic Bezier curves.

So how does it work?

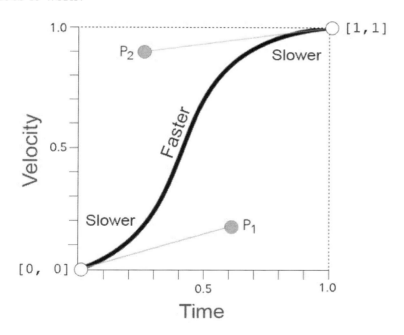

Figure 273: Two control points P1 and P2 are passed to `cubic-bezier` function as arguments. The range of values is between 0.0 and 1.0.

Because easing is determined by an equation, you can supply your own arguments to create unique curves to achieve a particular type of velocity not available by the predefined values.

As shown in the charts below, you can recreate the standard set of values using `cubic-bezier` function:

```
.linear {
    animation-timing-function: cubic-bezier(0, 0, 1, 1);
}

.ease {
    animation-timing-function: cubic-bezier(0.25, 0.1, 0.25, 1);
}

.ease-in {
    animation-timing-function: cubic-bezier(0.42, 0, 1, 1);
}

.ease-out {
    animation-timing-function: cubic-bezier(0, 0, 0.58, 1);
}

.ease-in-out {
    animation-timing-function: cubic-bezier(0.42, 0, 0.58, 1);
}
```

If you need slightly different curve for your UI elements, try to play around with the values until you achieve the effect you're looking for.

23.8 animation-fill-mode

When an animation is not currently playing, it is set to *fill mode* state. The property `animation-fill-mode` fills a non-playing animation with a chosen set of properties, usually taken from first or last keyframes.

Possible values:

none
Do not apply any styles to the animated element before or after animation is executing.

forwards
Retain styles from the last keyframe (can be affected by `animation-direction` and `animation-iteration-count`.)

backwards
Get styles from the first keyframe (can be affected by `animation-direction`), also retain this style during `animation-delay` state.

both
Extend animation properties in both directions (`forwards` and `backwards`.)

23.9 animation-play-state

Property `animation-play-state` specifies whether animation is running or paused.

Possible values:

paused
Animation is paused.

running
Animation is currently playing

For example, you can pause animation on mouse hover:

```
div:hover {
    animation-play-state: paused;
}
```

24 Forward & Inverse Kinematics

There isn't any *out-of-the-box* support for Inverse Kinematics in CSS. But, the effect can be simulated by using transform: `rotate(degree)` and `transform-origin` property to specify the pivot point between a parent and a child element.

Forward and Inverse Kinematics is the idea of translating rotation angle across multiple objects attached to each other at a pivot point. Kinematics are often used in simulating physics in video games. But we can use the same principle for animating 2D characters.

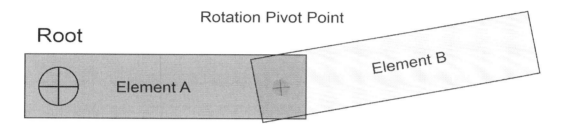

Figure 274: The **Root** point is the place where the primary element is attached to either another parent element, or an imaginary static point in space. If **Element A** moves, it must affect **Element B**, in such way as if they were attached to each other at a **Rotation Pivot Point**. This means, calculating all kinds of angles and lengths using trigonometric formulas. We can do this with JavaScript, or by using an existing vector / trigonometry library. But luckily, CSS already provides support for these types of element dynamics via the native `transform-origin` property.

Forward Kinematics is when by moving **Element A** the movement of **Element B** is also affected (*like a chain reaction*) as though they are attached to each other at a shared pivot point.

Inverse Kinematics is the reverse of that: the physical movement of **Element B** affects **Element A** provided that it's attached to some static point or another parent element. If not, the two elements can float in space :)

This is a lot like bone joints in an animated character!

25 Sassy CSS / SCSS Manual

In this chapter we will start from simple SCSS principles and build on them toward advanced directives. You can't really appreciate the power of Sassy CSS until you create your first *for-loop* in CSS.

You can even write your own sine and cosine (trigonometry) functions entirely using Sass/SCSS syntax.

Since we know that they depend on the value of `PI`. No problem! Sass variables can store floating point numbers, too: `$PI: 3.14159265359;`

Why would you want to do that? Surprisingly, knowing trigonometry (even at its basic level) can be of tremendous help when crafting your own animated UI elements. Especially when animation or rotation are involved.

But we'll get there in a moment. This manual was created help get familiar with the most important parts of Sass/SCSS. So let's begin!

25.1 New Syntax

SCSS doesn't really add any new features to CSS language, just new syntax that can, in many cases, shorten the amount of time spent writing CSS code.

In this chapter we will explore the new additions to CSS language syntax that Sassy CSS brings to the table.

This is not a complete Sass / SCSS manual. But to start taking primary advantages of Sass, you don't need to know everything about it. Just its key points. They will be explored in the following sections of this chapter.

In some cases SCSS and Sass will be used interchangeably, although there are slight syntax differences. However, primarily we will focus on SCSS.

All Sass/SCSS code compiles back to standard CSS, so the browser can actually understand and render the results. (*Browsers currently don't have direct support for Sass/SCSS, or any other CSS pre-processor.*)

25.2 Prerequisites

CSS pre-processors add new features to the *syntax* of CSS language.

There are 5 CSS pre-processors: **Sass**, **SCSS**, **Less**, **Stylus**, and **PostCSS**.

This entire chapter covers only SCSS, which is similar to Sass. But you can learn more about Sass at `www.sass-lang.com` website.

SASS – (`.sass`) – Syntactically Awesome Style Sheets.

SCSS – (`.scss`) – Sassy Cascading Style Sheets.

Extensions `.sass` and `.scss` are similar but not the same. For command line enthusiasts out there, you can convert from `.sass` to `.scss` and back:

```
# Convert Sass to SCSS
$ sass-convert style.sass style.scss

# Convert SCSS to Sass
$ sass-convert style.scss style.sass
```

Figure 275: Convert files between `.scss` and `.sass` formats, using Sass pre-processor command `sass-convert`.

SASS was the first specification for Sassy CSS with file extension `.sass`. The development started in 2006. But later an alternative syntax was developed with extension `.scss`, which some developers believe to be a better one.

There is currently no *out-of-the-box* support for Sassy CSS in any browser, regardless of which Sass syntax or extension you would use. But you can openly experiment with any of the 5 pre-processors on `codepen.io`. Aside from that you have to install a favorite CSS pre-processor on your web server.

This chapter was created to help you become familiar with SCSS. Other pre-processors share similar features, but the syntax may be different.

25.3 Superset

Sassy CSS in any of its manifestations is a superset of the CSS language. This means, everything that works in CSS will still work in Sass or SCSS.

25.4 Variables

Sass/SCSS allows you to work with variables. They are different from CSS variables that start with double dash (`--var-color`) we've seen earlier in this book. Instead they start with a dollar sign `$`:

code examples/sass/sass-variables.png

```
001 $number: 1;
002 $color: #FF0000;
003 $text: "Piece of string."
004 $text: "Another string." !default;
005 $nothing: null;
```

Figure 276: Basic variable definitions.

You can try to overwrite a variable name. If `!default` is appended to variable re-definition, and the variable already exists, it is not re-assigned again.

In other words, this means that the final value of variable `$text` from this example will still be *"Piece of string."*.

The second assignment *"Another string."* is ignored, because default value already exists.

code examples/sass/sass-container.png

```
001 #container {
002     content: $text;
003 }
```

Figure 277: Sass variables can be assigned to any CSS property.

25.5 Nested Rules

With Standard CSS, nested elements are accessed via space character.

```
001  /* Standard CSS */
002  #A {
003      color: red;
004  }
005
006  #A #B {
007      color: green;
008  }
009
010  #A #B #C p {
011      color: blue;
012  }
```

Figure 278: Nesting with standard CSS.

The above code can be expressed with Sassy's Nested Rules as follows:

```
001  /* Nested Rules */
002  #A {
003      color: red;
004      #B {
005          color: green;
006          #C p {
007              color: blue;
008          }
009      }
010  }
```

Figure 279: Nested Rules.

As you can see this syntax appears cleaner and less repetitious.

This is in particular helpful for managing complex layouts. This way the align in which nested CSS properties are written in code closely matches the actual structure of the application layout.

Behind the veil the pre-processor still compiles this to the standard CSS (*shown above,*) code so it can actually be rendered in the browser. We simply change the way we *write* CSS.

25.6 The & character

Sassy CSS adds the & (and) character directive.

Let's take a look at how it works!

code examples/sass/mixin-and-character.png

```
001  #P {
002      color: black;
003      a {
004          font-weight: bold;
005          &:hover {
006              color: red;
007          }
008      }
009  }
```

Figure 280: On line 5 the & character was used to specify &:hover and converted to the name of the parent element (a) after compilation.

code examples/sass/mixin-and-character-compiled.png

```
#P { color: black; }
#P a { font-weight: bold; }
#P a:hover { color: red; } // & was compiled to a (parent)
```

Figure 281: The & character is simply converted to the name of the parent element and becomes a:hover in this case.

25.7 Mixins

A mixin is defined by `@mixin` directive.

Let's create our first `@mixin` that defines default Flex behavior:

```
@mixin flexible() {
    display: flex;
    justify-content: center;
    align-items: center;
}

.centered-elements {
    @include flexible();
    border: 1px solid gray;
}
```

Figure 282: Now every time you apply `.centered-elements` class to an HTML element it will turn into Flexbox. One of the key benefits of mixins is that you can use them together with other CSS properties. Here I also added `border:1px solid gray;` to `.centered-elements` in addition to the mixin.

You can even pass arguments to a `@mixin` as if it were a function, and then assign them to CSS properties. We'll take a look at that in the next section.

25.8 Multiple Browsers Example

Some experimental features (such as *-webkit-based*) or Firefox (*-moz-based*) only work in browsers in which they appear.

Mixins can be helpful in defining browser-specific CSS properties in one class.

For example, if you need to rotate an element in Webkit-based browsers, as well as the other ones, you can create this mixin that takes `$degree` argument:

code examples/sass/mixin-3-rotate.png

```
@mixin rotate($degree) {
    -webkit-transform: rotate($degree); // Webkit-based
    -moz-transform: rotate($degree);    // Firefox
    -ms-transform: rotate($degree);     // Internet Explorer
    -o-transform: rotate($degree);      // Opera
    transform: rotate($degree);         // Standard CSS
}
```

Figure 283: Browser-agnostic `@mixin` for specifying angle of rotation.

Now all we have to do is `@include` this mixin in our CSS class definition:

code examples/sass/mixin-4.png

```
.rotate-element {
    @include rotate(45deg);
}
```

Figure 284: Rotate in compliance with all browsers.

25.9 Arithmetic Operators

Similar to standard CSS syntax, you can ***add***, ***subtract***, ***multiple*** and ***divide*** values, without having to use the `calc()` function from the classic CSS syntax (*See an earlier chapter on how to add values using* `calc()` *function.*)

But there are a few non-obvious cases that might produce errors.

25.9.1 Addition

code examples/sass/sass-add.png

```
p {
    font-size: 10px + 2em; // *error: incompatible units
    font-size: 10px + 6px; // 16px
    font-size: 10px + 6;   // 16px
}
```

Figure 285: Adding values without using `calc()` function. Just make sure that both values are provided in a matching format.

25.9.2 Subtraction

Subtraction operator (-) works in the same exact way as addition.

code examples/sass/sass-subtract.png

```
001  div {
002      height: 12% - 2%;
003      margin: 4rem - 1;
004  }
```

Figure 286: Subtracting different type of values.

25.9.3 Multiplication

code examples/sass/sass-multiplcation-division.png

```
001  p {
002      width: 10px * 10px;        // *error
003      width: 10px * 10;          // 100px
004      width: 1px * 5 + 5px;      // 10px
005      width: 5 * (5px + 5px);    // 50px
006      width: 5px + (10px / 2) * 3; // 20px
007  }
```

Figure 287: Multiplication and Division (*last example*).

25.9.4 Division

Division is a bit tricky. Because in standard CSS, the division symbol is reserved for using together with some short-hand properties. And SCSS claims to be compatible with standard CSS.

code examples/sass/sass-css-slash.png

```
001  p { font: 16px / 24px Arial, sans-serif; }
```

In standard CSS, division symbol appears in *short-hand* `font` property. But it isn't used to actually divide values. So, how does Sass handle division?

```
001 p {
002     top: 16px / 24px          // Outputs as classic CSS
003     top: (16px / 24px)        // Does division (when parentheses are added)
004     top: #{$var1} / #{$var2}; // Uses interpolation, outputs as CSS
005     top: $var1 / $var2;       // Does division
006     top: random(4) / 5;       // Does division (when paired with function)
007     top: 2px / 4px + 3px      // Does division (when part of arithmetic)
008 }
```

Figure 288: If you want to divide two values, simply add parenthesis around the division operation. Otherwise, division will work only in combination with some of the other operators or functions.

25.9.5 Remainder

The remainder calculates the remainder of the division operation. In this example, let's see how it can be used to create a zebra stripe pattern for an arbitrary set of HTML elements.

```
001 @mixin zebra() {
002     @for $i from 1 through 7 {
003         @if ($i % 2 == 1) {
004             .stripe-#{$i} {
005                 background-color: black;
006                 color: white;
007             }
008         }
009     }
010 }
011
012 * { @include zebra(); }
```

Figure 289: Let's start with creating a zebra mixin. **Note:** the `@for` and `@if` rules are discussed in a following section.

This demo requires at least a few HTML elements:

```
001  <div class = "stripe-1">zebra</div>
002  <div class = "stripe-2">zebra</div>
003  <div class = "stripe-3">zebra</div>
004  <div class = "stripe-4">zebra</div>
005  <div class = "stripe-5">zebra</div>
006  <div class = "stripe-6">zebra</div>
007  <div class = "stripe-7">zebra</div>
```

Figure 290: HTML source code for this mixin experiment.

And here is the browser outcome:

Figure 291: Zebra stripe generated by the zebra `@mixin`.

25.9.6 Comparison Operators

code examples/sass/sass-condition.png

Operator	Example	Description
==	x == y	returns true if x and y are equal
!=	x != y	returns true if x and y are not equal
>	x > y	returns true if x is greater than y
<	x < y	returns true if x is less than y
>=	x >= y	returns true if x is greater than or equal to y
<=	x <= y	returns true if x is less than or equal to y

Figure 292: Comparison Operators.

How can comparison operators be used in practice? We can try to write a `@mixin` that will choose padding sizing if its greater than margin:

code examples/sass/sass-spacing-example.png

```
@mixin spacing($padding, $margin) {
    @if ($padding > $margin) {
        padding: $padding;
    } @else {
        padding: $margin;
    }
}

.container {
    @include spacing(10px, 20px);
}
```

Figure 293: Comparison operators in action.

After compiling we will arrive at this CSS:

code examples/sass/sass-condit-result.png
```
001 .container { padding: 20px; }
```

Figure 294: Result of the conditional spacing @mixin.

25.9.7 Logical Operators

code examples/sass/sass-logical-operators.png

Operator	Example	Description
and	x and y	returns true if x and y are true
or	x or y	returns true if x or y is true
not	not x	returns true if x is not true

Figure 295: Logical Operators.

code examples/sass/sass-mixin-button-color-1.png
```
001 @mixin button-color($height, $width) {
002     @if(($height < $width) and ($width >= 35px)) {
003         background-color: blue;
004     } @else {
005         background-color: green;
006     }
007 }
008
009 .button {
010     @include button-color(20px, 30px)
011 }
```

Figure 296: Using Sass Logical Operators, to create a button color class that changes its background color based on its width.

25.9.8 Strings

In some cases it is possible to add strings to valid non-quoted CSS values, as long as the added string is trailing:

code examples/sass/sass-string-0.png

```
001  p {
002      font: 50px Ari + "al";  // Compiles to 50px Arial
003  }
```

Figure 297: Combining regular CSS property values with Sass/SCSS strings.

The following example, on the other hand will produce compilation error:

code examples/sass/sass-string-00.png

```
001  p {
002      font: "50px " + Arial;  // Error
003  }
```

Figure 298: This example will not work

You can add strings together without double quotes, as long as the string doesn't contain spaces. For example, the following example will not compile:

code examples/sass/sass-string-3.png

```
001  p:after {
002      content: "Quoted string with " + added tail.;
003  }
```

Figure 299: This example will not work, either

Solution?

code examples/sass/sass-string-4.png

```
p:after {
    content: "Quoted string with " + "added tail.";
}
```

Figure 300: Strings containing spaces must be wrapped in quotes.

code examples/sass/sass-string-5.png

```
p:after {
    content: "Long " + "String " + "Added";
}
```

Figure 301: Adding multiple strings.

code examples/sass/sass-string-6.png

```
p:after {
    content: "Long " + 1234567 + "Added";
}
```

Figure 302: Adding numbers and strings.

Note, `content` property works only with pseudo selectors `:before` and `:after`. It is recommended to avoid using `content` property in your CSS definitions. Always specify content between HTML tags. Here, it is explained only in context of working with strings in Sass/SCSS.

25.10 Control-Flow Statements

SCSS has **functions()** and **@directives**. We've already created a type of a function when we looked at mixins you could pass arguments to. A function usually has a parenthesis appended to the end of the function's name. A directive starts with an @ character.

Just like in JavaScript or other languages, SCSS lets you work with the standard set of *control-flow* statements.

25.10.1 if()

`if()` is a function.

The usage is rather primitive. The statement will return one of the two specified values, based on a condition:

```
001  /* Using if() function */
002  if(true, 1px, 2px)  => 1px
003  if(false, 1px, 2px) => 2px
```

25.10.2 @if

`@if` is a directive used to branch out based on a condition.

```
001  /* Using @if directive */
002  p {
003      @if 1 + 1 == 2  { border: 1px solid;  }
004      @if 7 < 5       { border: 2px dotted; }
005      @if null        { border: 3px double; }
006  }
```

This Sassy *if-statement* compiles to:

```
001  p { border: 1px solid; }
```

code examples/sass/sass-if-if-else.png

```
/* Create a variable $type */
$type: river;

/* Paint divs blue if variable is set to river */
div {
    @if $type == river {
        color: blue;
    }
}

/* Conditional colors on paragraph */
p {
    @if $type == tree {
        color: green;
    } @else if $type == river {
        color: blue;
    } @else if $type == dirt {
        color: brown;
    }
}
```

Figure 303: Example of using a single `if`-*statement* or an `if-else` combo.

Checking If Parent Exists

The AND symbol (&) will select the parent element, if it exists. Or return `null` otherwise. Therefore, it can be used in combination with an `@if` directive.

In the following examples, let's take a look at how we can create *conditional* CSS styles based on whether the parent element exists or not.

code examples/sass/sass-does-parent-exist.png

```
/* Check if parent exists */
@mixin does-parent-exist {
    @if & {
        /* Apply color blue to parent if it exists */
        &:hover {
            color: blue;
        }
    } @else {
        /* Parent doesn't exist, apply blue to links */
        a {
            color: blue;
        }
    }
}

p {
    @include does-parent-exist();
}
```

Figure 304: If parent doesn't exist & evaluates to `null`, and an alternative style will be used.

25.10.3 @for

The `@for` directive can be used for repeating CSS definitions multiple times in a row.

code examples/sass/sass-for-loop.png
```
@for $i from 1 through 5 {
    .definition-#{$i} { width: 10px * $i; }
}
```

Figure 305: A for loop iterating over 5 items.

This loop will compile into the following CSS:

code examples/sass/sass-for-loop-compiled.png
```
.definition-1 { width: 10px; }
.definition-2 { width: 20px; }
.definition-3 { width: 30px; }
.definition-4 { width: 40px; }
.definition-5 { width: 50px; }
```

Figure 306: Outcome of the for loop.

25.10.4 @each

The `@each` directive can be used for iterating over a list of values.

code examples/sass/sass-each.png
```
@each $animal in platypus, lion, sheep, dove {
    .#{$animal}-icon {
        background-image: url("/images/#{$animal}.png");
    }
}
```

Figure 307: Iteating over a set of values.

This code will be compiled to the following CSS:

code examples/sass/sass-each-compiled.png
```
001 .platypus-icon {
002     background-image: url("/images/platypus}.png");
003 }
004 .lion-icon {
005     background-image: url("/images/lion.png");
006 }
007 .sheep-icon {
008     background-image: url("/images/sheep.png");
009 }
010 .dove-icon {
011     background-image: url("/images/dove.png");
012 }
```

Figure 308: Compiled animal icons.

25.10.5 @while

code examples/sass/sass-while-10.png
```
001 $index: 5;
002 @while $index > 0 {
003     .element-#{$index} { width: 10px * $index; }
004     $index: $index - 1;
005 }
```

Figure 309: While loop.

code examples/sass/sass-while-html-elements.png
```
001 .element-5 { width: 50px; }
002 .element-4 { width: 40px; }
003 .element-3 { width: 30px; }
004 .element-2 { width: 20px; }
005 .element-1 { width: 10px; }
```

Figure 310: Listing of 5 HTML elements produced by while loop.

25.11 Sass Functions

Using Sass / SCSS you can define functions just like in any other language.

Let's create a function `three-hundred-px` that returns value of `300px`.

code examples/sass/sass-function-example.png

```
@function three-hundred-px() {
    @return 300px;
}

.name {
    width: three-hundred-px();
    border: 1px solid gray;
    display: block;
    position: absolute;
}
```

Figure 311: Example of a function that returns a value.

code examples/sass/sass-div-hello.png

```
<div class = "name">Hello.</div>
```

When the class `.name` is applied to an element, a width of `300px` will be applied to it:

code examples/sass/sass-hello-simple.png

Hello.

Of course Sass functions can return any valid CSS value, and assigned to any CSS property you can think of. They can even be calculated, based on a passed argument:

code examples/sass/sass-function-return-double.png

```
@function double($width) {
    return $width * 2;
}
```

25.12 Sass Trigonometry

Trigonometry functions `sin` and `cos` are often found as part of built-in classes in many languages, such as JavaScript, for example.

I think learning how they work is worth it, if you're looking to reduce the time taken to design UI animations (Let's say a spinning progress bar, for example.)

Toward the end of this chapter, I will demonstrate a couple of examples that reduce code to a minimum for creating interesting animation effects using the `sin()` function. The same principles can be expanded upon to be used for creating interactive UI elements.

Using trigonometry together with CSS is a great way to reduce bandwidth. Instead of using `.gif` animations (*each might take an extra HTTP request to load, since* `.gif` *animations cannot be placed into a single image.*)

You can write your own trigonometry functions in Sass.

25.13 Writing your own functions in Sass

This section was included to demonstrate how to write your own functions in Sass/SCSS.

In trigonometry many operations are based on these functions. They all build on top of each other. For example, the `rad()` function requires `PI()`. The `cos()` and `sin()` functions require `rad()` function.

code examples/sass/sass-trig-functions-1.png
```
001  @function PI() { @return 3.14159265359; }
```

Writing functions in Sass/SCSS feels a lot like writing them in JavaScript or similar programming languages.

code examples/sass/sass-trig-functions-2.png
```
001 @function pow($number, $exp) {
002   $value: 1;
003   @if $exp > 0 {
004     @for $i from 1 through $exp {
005       $value: $value * $number;
006     }
007   }
008   @else if $exp < 0 {
009     @for $i from 1 through -$exp {
010       $value: $value / $number;
011     }
012   }
013   @return $value;
014 }
```

code examples/sass/sass-trig-functions-3.png
```
001 @function rad($angle) {
002   $unit: unit($angle);
003   $unitless: $angle / ($angle * 0 + 1);
004   // If angle has 'deg' as unit convert to radians.
005   @if $unit == deg {
006     $unitless: $unitless / 180 * PI();
007   }
008   @return $unitless;
009 }
```

code examples/sass/sass-trig-functions-4.png
```
001 @function sin($angle) {
002   $sin: 0;
003   $angle: rad($angle);
004   // Iterate 10 times.
005   @for $i from 0 through 10 {
006     $fact =fact(2 * $i + 1);
007     $pow = pow($angle, (2 * $i + 1)) / $fact;
008     $sin: $sin + pow(-1, $i) * ;
009   }
010   @return $sin;
011 }
```

code examples/sass/sass-trig-functions-5.png

```
001  @function cos($angle) {
002    $cos: 0;
003    $angle: rad($angle);
004    // Iterate a bunch of times.
005    @for $i from 0 through 10 {
006      $pow = pow($angle, 2 * $i);
007      $cos: $cos + pow(-1, $i) * $pow / fact(2 * $i);
008    }
009    @return $cos;
010  }
```

Finally, to calculate *tangent* using the `tan()` function, the functions `sin()` and `cos()` are required components.

code examples/sass/sass-trig-functions-6.png

```
001  @function tan($angle) {
002    @return sin($angle) / cos($angle);
003  }
```

If writing your own math and trigonometry functions isn't exciting, you can simply include **compass** library (*see next example*) and start using `sin()`, `cos()` and other trig functions out of the box.

25.14 Oscillator Animation

Let's take everything we learned from this chapter to put together a sinusoid oscillator animation.

code examples/sass/sass-oscillator.png
```
001 @import "compass/css3";
002
003 .atom {
004     text-align:    center;
005     border-radius: 20px;
006     height:        40px;
007     width:         40px;
008     margin:        1px;
009     display:       inline-block;
010     border:        10px #1893E7 solid;
011     /* Apply oscillate animation (defined below) */
012     animation: oscillate 3s ease-in-out infinite;
013     /* Create 15 classes for each of the 15 boxes */
014     @for $i from 1 through 15 {
015         &:nth-child(#{$i}) {
016             animation-delay: ( #{sin(.4) * ($i)}s );
017         }
018     }
019 }
020
021 @keyframes oscillate {
022     0%  { transform: translateY(0px);   }
023     50% { transform: translateY(200px); }
024 }
```

Figure 312: Combining everything we know about Sassy CSS and CSS Animations explored in one of the previous chapters.

code examples/sass/div-class-atom-15-times.png
```
001 <!-- Repeat this element 15 times //-->
002 <div class = "atom"></div>
```

Figure 313: The HTML part. This is a shortened example. Make sure to have 15 actual HTML elements with `class = "atom"`.

Finally, the result of this operation will produce the following animation:

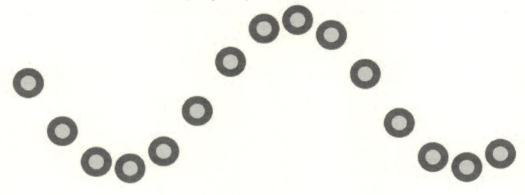

Figure 314: The result of previous code – an *animated* oscillating sin wave.

All of this has taken us roughly less than 24 lines of code!

Note: If you are using the Vue framework, you can render all 15 elements using this simple **for-loop** via the **v-for** directive – instead of typing out all 15 HTML elements by hand – further reducing the hassle.

code examples/sass/sass-trig-functions-vue-1.png
```
001  <ul id = "atoms">
002    <li v-for = "atom in atoms">
003      {{ atom.message }}
004    </li>
005  </ul>
```

Figure 315: Setup for listing 15 HTML elements with just few lines of code in Vue framework.

code examples/sass/sass-trig-functions-vue-2.png
```
001  let atoms = new Vue({
002    el: "#atoms",
003    data: {
004      atoms: new Array(15).fill(0);
005    }
006  });
```

Figure 316: JavaScript Vue object, that creates an Array object and fill it with 15 items containing value "0".

I included it here just to show how combining multiple frameworks and libraries, your code becomes easier to write and maintain in the future.

Though, that is not to say you should use them in every single project. Sometimes it's easier to write out the code in simple vanilla form.

Working professionally, though, chances are you will encounter a build using multiple libraries.

26 Tesla CSS Art

Although CSS language was designed primarily for helping with the creation of websites and web application layouts, some talented UI designers have pushed it to its absolute limit! Some argue that there is little practical use in doing this. But the fact remains... these artists create challenging designs using deep knowledge of CSS properties and values.

Below is a CSS model of Tesla in space, designed by Sasha Tran (@sa_sha26 on Twitter) exclusively for this book!

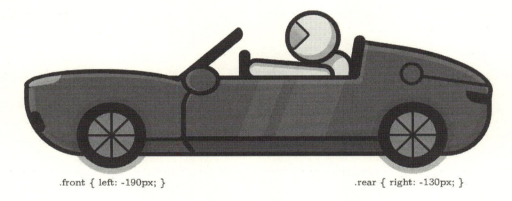

Figure 317: Tesla in space, designed entirely in CSS by Sasha Tran (@sa_sha26) you should follow her on Twitter if you want to stay in touch with a talented UI designer!

The remaining pages of this book will describe, in great detail, how each separate part of this car was created, which CSS properties were used, etc.

Making CSS art can be a challenge, even for web designers. We're taking everything we've learned so far in this book and putting it into action!

It's all about how skillful you are with the CSS properties: `overflow:hidden`, `transform:rotate`, `box-shadow` and `border-radius`.

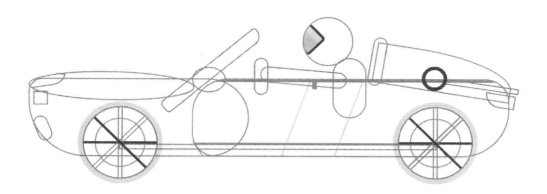

Figure 318: By making all backgrounds transparent you can clearly see the Tesla's composition, consisting of several HTML `<div>` elements.

On the pages that follow we'll break down each significant element of the car to demonstrate how it was created.

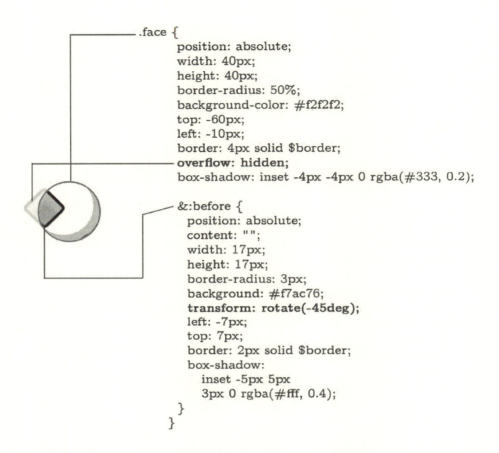

```
.face {
    position: absolute;
    width: 40px;
    height: 40px;
    border-radius: 50%;
    background-color: #f2f2f2;
    top: -60px;
    left: -10px;
    border: 4px solid $border;
    overflow: hidden;
    box-shadow: inset -4px -4px 0 rgba(#333, 0.2);

    &:before {
      position: absolute;
      content: "";
      width: 17px;
      height: 17px;
      border-radius: 3px;
      background: #f7ac76;
      transform: rotate(-45deg);
      left: -7px;
      top: 7px;
      border: 2px solid $border;
      box-shadow:
         inset -5px 5px
         3px 0 rgba(#fff, 0.4);
    }
}
```

Figure 319: The helmet consists of a circle and the orange face shield which is just a *nested*, rotated square with white *inner* box shadow, that cuts off at the radius line because `.face` is set to `overflow:hidden`.

Note how `&:before` is *nested* inside `.face` using { brackets }. This is accomplished by using the SASS extension (Syntactically Awesome Style Sheets). I recommend looking more into it at http://sass-lang.com. It is also briefly discussed at the very beginning of this book.

Of course you can still rewrite this in standard vanilla CSS by replacing `&:before` and the brackets by a separate element with its own **id** or **class**.

```scss
&-bumper-top {
    width: 135px;
    height: 23px;
    position: absolute;
    background-color: $car-body;
    border: 4px solid;
    border-radius: 50%;
    top: -8px;
    left: -235px;
    transform: rotate(1deg);
    border-color: $border transparent transparent $border;
    overflow: hidden;
    z-index: 99;
    box-shadow: inset 0 3px 0 rgba(#fff, 0.17);

    .front-light-bulb {
        position: absolute;
        width: 33px;
        height: 10px;
        background:
            rgba(#fff, 0.5);
        transform:
            rotate(-10deg);
        border-radius: 50px 0;
        left: -4px;
        top: 1px;
    }
}
```

Figure 320: The hood is a long oval element rotated by just 1 degree. In the same way as the helmet's face shield, the light bulb is hidden within the parent by using `overflow:hidden`. Hiding the overflow is what helps us get away with creating more complex, irregular shapes that closely describe real-life objects.

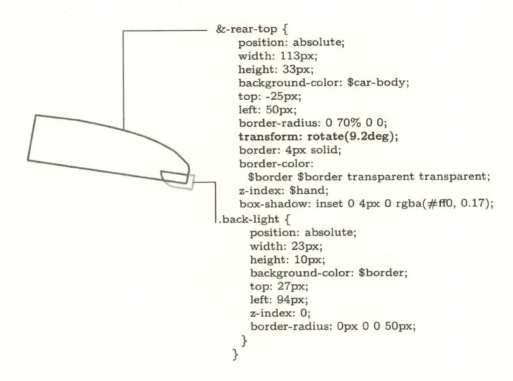

Figure 321: The importance of `overflow:hidden` in creating CSS art cannot be understated. The back light is using absolutely the same technique as the previous two examples. The back of the car is a *rotated* rectangle with just one of the corners rounded. Here you just have to follow your artist's instinct, in order to create shapes that match your preference and a sense of style.

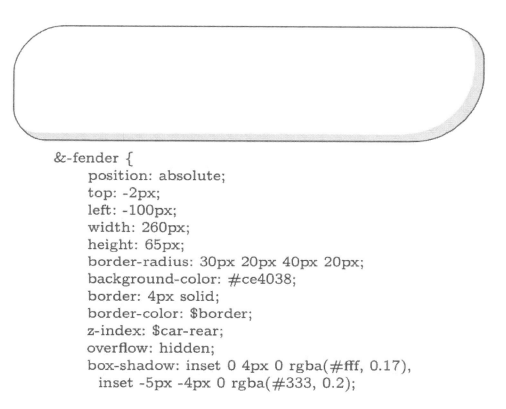

```
&-fender {
    position: absolute;
    top: -2px;
    left: -100px;
    width: 260px;
    height: 65px;
    border-radius: 30px 20px 40px 20px;
    background-color: #ce4038;
    border: 4px solid;
    border-color: $border;
    z-index: $car-rear;
    overflow: hidden;
    box-shadow: inset 0 4px 0 rgba(#fff, 0.17),
       inset -5px -4px 0 rgba(#333, 0.2);
```

Figure 322: The base of the car that stretches toward its back is simply a large rectangular `div` element with rounded corners and an *inner* `box-shadow`.

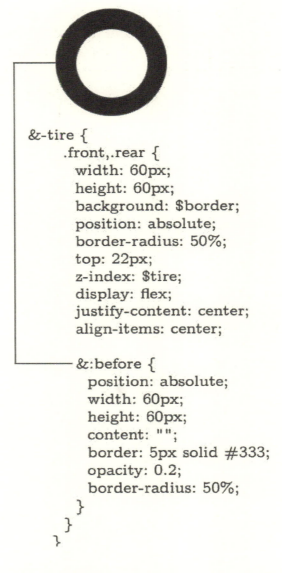

Figure 323: Again using SCSS here, the & stands for "this" (conceptually similar to "this" object in JavaScript) meaning... the element is referring to itself. As we have seen in one of the chapters of this book, the :before (and also :after) pseudo-selectors are actually contained within the same HTML element. They can be used to create additional shapes, without having to nest more elements.

And there you have it! I've only talked about the key CSS properties often used to create CSS art. To avoid redundancy some of the most obvious ones were skipped. For example, it is assumed you already know how to use `top`, `left`, `width` and `height` properties.

To see the original CSS code for the Tesla on `codepen.io` visit the following URL:

`https://codepen.io/sashatran/pen/gvVWKJ`

Figure 324: This artwork was created with CSS.

Figure 325: Another CSS painting by **Diana A Smith**. You can view it in your browser at http://diana-adrianne.com/purecss-zigario/

Credits

It is rare for a book to be written entirely by a single person. While all diagrams were created by the author of this book, this volume would not be possible without contributions of other talented artists, graphic designers and editors. Their names are listed in this section. I'm thankful to have a team of contributors and volunteers who, after several editorial iterations, have collectively helped make this book be what it is today.

Thanks To

Sasha Tran *Front End Developer* for contributing the CSS rendition of the Tesla and complete CSS source code. If you like her CSS art work, you can get a hold of her via her website ***sashatran.com***, her *Codepen.io* account at ***https://codepen.io/sashatran/*** or on Twitter ***@sa_sha26***.

Katya Sorok *Editor* for pointing out numerous improvements to text and images found in this book. Her Twitter username is ***@KSorok***.

Fabio Di Corleto *Graphic Designer* for contributing the original concept work for the Tesla in space image. If you're looking for a talented Graphic Designer you can get in touch with him at ***fabiodicorleto@gmail.com*** or via his *Instagram* and Dribbble pages. His username ***fabiodicorleto*** is the same across his social media accounts.

Special Thanks To

Diana A Smith *UI Engineer* for creating incredible CSS artwork. If you want to see the upper limit of CSS rendering capabilities in the latest version of Chrome browser, I can't recommend this enough – you should definitely check out this website: ***http://diana-adrianne.com*** There is simply no other original CSS art of this type that exists elsewhere on the Internet.

Index

:after, 39, 74, 236
:before, 39, 74, 236
:first, 27
:hover, 65
:last, 27
:nth-child, 25, 26
%, 49, 97
0.5fr, 162
1fr, 161
2d Transforms, 117
2d transforms, 117
3D Transforms, 121
3D cube, 124

absolute, 40, 54
access via javascript, 111
align, 126
align-items, 134, 135
align-self, 181
animation, 189, 191
animation easing types, 196
animation pivot point, 202
animation-delay, 191, 193
animation-direction, 194
animation-duration, 191, 192
animation-fill-mode, 191
animation-iteration-count, 191, 195
animation-name, 191, 192
animation-play-state, 191
animation-timing-function, 191, 196
area names, 184
arial, 48
auto, 155

automatic width, 154

baackground-attachment:fixed, 107
backface-visibility, 125
background, 95
Background Images, 94
background-attachment, 107
background-attachment:scroll, 107
background-color, 231
background-image, 94, 95
background-origin, 108
background-position, 100
background-position:center center, 100
background-repeat, 95
background-repeat:no-repeat, 95, 99
background-repeat:repeat-x, 101
background-repeat:repeat-y, 101
background-size, 96
background-size: top left, 96
background-size:100%, 99
background-size:100% 100%, 99
background:100%, 97
basis, 136
bezier, 196
bezier curve, 196
block, 76
bold, 48
border, 35, 231
Border Radius, 65
border-bottom-left-radius, 112–114
border-bottom-right-radius, 112–114

border-box, 36, 37, 108
border-radius, 65, 72, 73, 112–114, 229, 231
border-top-left-radius, 112–114
border-top-right-radius, 112–114
Borders, 111
Bottom, 184
bottom, 40, 109
BottomLeft, 184
BottomRight, 184
box model, 1, 35
Box Shadow, 65
box-radius, 68
box-shadow, 67, 68, 229, 231
box-sizing, 35, 36

cell, 154
cell width, 154
center, 133, 134
center center, 109
clear, 80
clear:both, 80
cmu bright, 48
cmu classical serif, 48
color, 48
Color Gradients, 81
column, 131, 134
common properties, 22
contain, 97, 110
content, 231
content-box, 36, 37, 108
cover, 97, 110
Creating Your First CSS Grid, 147
cross-axis, 126, 131
css animation, 189
css art, 229

CSS Box Model, 35
css filters, 91
CSS Grid, 141
css grid, 142
css grid and media queries, 145
css grid end, 174
css grid gaps, 155
css grid lines, 186
css grid spans, 170
css grid start, 174
css grid template areas, 142
css template areas, 142
css variables, 16
cube, 124

default position, 40
degrees, 118
Direction, 128
direction, 147
direction:rows, 147
Display, 76
display, 76
display:block, 69, 70, 76, 118
display:flex, 126
display:inline, 76
display:inline-block, 76
display:none, 79
Document Object Model, 19
DOM, 19
dotted, 56
double, 56

easing, 196
Element Visibility, 79
Elliptical Border Radius, 114
em, 49
end, 174

external code placement, 2
external css file, 2

fill, 110
filters, 91
fixed, 107
flex, 126, 137
flex cross-axis, 126
flex main-axis, 126
flex-basis, 136, 137
flex-direction, 127–129, 134
flex-direction:row, 129, 133
flex-direction:row-reverse, 128
flex-end, 133, 134
flex-flow, 129
flex-flow:row wrap, 129
flex-flow:row wrap-reverse, 129
flex-flow:row wrap;, 130
flex-flow:row-reverse wrap, 130
flex-flow:row-reverse wrap-reverse;, 130
flex-grow, 136, 137
flex-shrink, 137
flex-start, 133, 134
flex-wrap, 127–129, 131
flex-wrap:wrap, 128, 129
flex-wrap:wrap-reverse, 131
float, 80
float:left, 76, 80
float:right, 76, 80
Floating Elements, 80
Flow, 129
flow, 129
font features, 60
font-family, 48
font-feature-settings, 60

font-size, 48, 69, 70
font-style, 48
font-weight, 48
forward kinematics, 202
fr, 161
fr units, 163
fractional units, 161, 163

geometricPrecision, 57
glow effect, 68
glyph-orientation-horizontal, 60
glyph-orientation-vertical, 60
Gradient Types, 85
gradients, 81
grid, 141
grid area names, 184
grid cell, 154
grid gaps, 155
grid lines, 186
grid spans, 170
grid-auto-flow, 147
grid-auto-flow-column, 154
grid-auto-rows, 153
grid-column, 171, 173, 174, 178–180, 182
grid-column-end, 152, 175, 177
grid-column-start, 152, 175, 177
grid-column:span, 170, 173
grid-gap, 157, 158
grid-row, 171, 173, 174, 178–180, 182
grid-row-end, 152, 174, 175
grid-row-gap, 157
grid-row-span, 170
grid-row-start, 152, 174, 175, 177
grid-row:span, 173

grid-template-areas, 184
grid-template-columns, 148, 149, 155, 167, 169, 186
grid-template-columns:repeat, 169
grid-template-row, 186
grid-template-rows, 148, 149, 167, 186
grud-column-gap, 156

height, 231
hidden, 79
hierarchical animation, 202
hsl, 89

IK, 202
Image Transparency, 103
image.jpg, 94
implicit, 150
Implicit Columns, 150
Implicit Rows, 150
including external css file, 2
inline, 76
inline code placement, 4
inline css, 4
inline-block, 40, 76
internal code placement, 3
internal css, 3
inverse kinematics, 202
irregular shapes, 72
italic, 48

justify, 126
justify-content, 130, 133, 139
justify-content:space-between, 130
justify-items, 139
justify-self, 181, 183

kitten, 94

Left, 184
left, 40, 109, 231
left bottom, 109
left top, 109
liga, 60
ligatures, 60
line-height, 59, 61, 69, 70
line-through, 56
linear-gradient, 82, 85
local variables, 16

main-axis, 126
margin, 35, 66
margin-top, 66
Margins, 65
media queries, 145
Middle-of-Nowhere, 184
min-width, 136
Multiple Backgrounds, 102
multiple backgrounds, 104
multiple-backgrounds, 105

naming css grid lines, 186
Naming Grid Lines, 186
Nike Logo, 73
Nike logo, 73
no-repeat, 95
none, 79, 110
normal, 48

object-fit, 110
opacity, 236
optimizeLegibility, 57
optimizeSpeed, 57
order, 138
overflow, 54, 71–73, 232
overflow: hidden, 71

overflow:auto, 54
overflow:hidden, 55, 72, 110, 229, 231
overflow:scroll, 54
overflow:visible, 70, 110
overline, 56
Overview, 82

Packing flex lines, 134
padding, 35
padding-box, 36, 108
perspective, 121
perspective-origin, 121
position, 40
position:absolute, 66, 231
position:inline-block, 40
position:relative, 40, 66, 118
position:static, 40
Pseudo Classes, 25
Pseudo Selectors, 25
pt, 49
px, 49

radial-gradient, 82, 87
relative, 40
rendering text, 57
repeat, 169
repeat-x, 101
repeat-y, 101
Repeating Values, 169
repeating-linear-gradient, 82, 89
repeating-radial-gradient, 82, 89
Right, 184
right, 40, 109
right bottom, 109
right top, 109
rotate, 117, 118

rotate text, 63
rotateX, 121
rotateY, 122
rotateZ, 122
rotation degrees, 118
Rounded Corners, 65
row, 130
row-reverse, 130
rows, 147

sans-serif, 49
sass, 203
sassy css, 203
scale, 122
scroll, 107
SCSS, 235
scss, 203
selectors, 22
shorthand, 23
shorthand property names, 23
size, 49
skip ink, 56
space, 27
space character, 27
space-around, 133, 134
space-between, 130, 133, 134
space-evenly, 133, 134
span, 76, 173
Spans, 170
start, 174
static element position, 40
stretch, 133, 134
stretch background image, 99
SVG, 63
SVG text, 63

Template Areas, 184

template areas, 142
Tesla, 229
Tesla CSS art, 229
text, 48, 57
Text Shadow, 62
text-align, 52, 61
text-align-last, 52
text-align:center, 61, 76
text-anchor, 64
text-combine-upright, 53
text-decoration, 48, 57
text-decoration-skip-ink, 56, 57
text-direction, 133
text-indent, 58
text-orientation, 59
text-shadow, 62
times new roman, 49
Top, 184
top, 40, 109, 231
TopLeft, 184
TopRight, 184
transform, 231
transform-origin, 120, 202
transform-origin and animation, 202
transform-rotate, 231
transform:matrix, 123
transform:rotate, 229, 231

translate, 117, 118, 123
translateX, 123
translateY, 123
translateZ, 123

underline, 48, 56
upright, 59, 61
url, 94
url(image.jpg), 94
use-glyph-orientation, 60

variables, 16
verdana, 48
vertical-rl, 60
vertical=lr, 60
visibility, 79
visible, 79

wavy, 56
width, 231
Working With Fractional Units, 163
Wrap, 128
wrap, 128, 130
wrap-reverse, 129–131
writing-mode, 53, 60

Z-Index, 65
z-index, 67

Made in the USA
Middletown, DE
28 March 2019